I0491418

Who Can Best Work and Best Agree?

A 21st Century Approach for Inclusion and Growth in the Lodge

Charles Matulewicz

"He is a wise man who does not grieve for the things which he has not but rejoices for those which he has."

Epictetus

Dedication

This text is dedicated to the Brothers who work Tirelessly to Improve their Lodges for Brothers who have not yet knocked on the West Gate.

And more especially my friend and Brother RW Ken Taylor. If my Grandfather Worshipful Brother George Conover inspired me to consider Masonry, and my dear friend RW Brother Edward Kraft inspired me to get involved in Masonry you my friend showed me that Masonry was bigger than me and inspired me to leave Masonry better than I found it.

And to Amanda, my wife, who supports me in my Masonic work, despite many failed attempts to not to wake her up when I return late from Lodge…

Forward

For the past several years now, it has been one of my favorite pastimes to spend time in fellowship with my masonic Brother, Charles Matulewicz. Although we are from different backgrounds, lodges, educational levels and, I suspect, differing political opinions, our love for this fraternity and for wanting it to succeed and survive has been something that has been a bond that has led us to many extended and heartfelt conversations on the subject.

I first met Charles at Palestine Lodge #189 in my hometown of Catonsville, Maryland shortly after he was raised in 2008. He's the type of man that, when you meet him, you know that there is something different and special about this individual. His smile, charm and wit have an uncanny ability to engage you in conversations which will inevitably lead you to give much deeper thought to subjects that you have pondered before but hardly to this extent. Such is the way it goes when the subject turns to preserving our gentle craft. In this, his second book, Brother Matulewicz gives the reader the benefit of his keen insights on the problems of modern-day Masonry, some of the causes and gives a path forward to helping improve the Blue Lodge experience and thus improving Masonry in general.

From the early pages, where he uses scenarios, both real and imaginary, to exemplify how the teaching of some of our emblems relate to real life applications, he begins to exhibit the difference between "members" and "masons", which is one of the important distinctions pointed out in this work. The experience and knowledge that Brother Charles has amassed during his time as a Mason is the result of his experience, study, hard work and dedication. He has served his lodges as Worshipful Master six times, I can say from observing that during his time as WM of Palestine Lodge, the excitement and activity of that lodge was legendary, and it was an absolute pleasure to fellowship with the brethren on those lodge nights. Charles was the "Dean" of the Maryland Masonic Academy when it was first instituted back in 2016 and was the author of the curriculum and text for the Fellow of the Craft and Pillar of the Craft programs leading up to induction into "King Solomon's Society".

He has also served the Grand Lodge as a Grand Steward and Grand Inspector. I mention these things to let you know that the material included in this book is based on a long masonic career of educating others in the meaning, law and esoteric qualities of Masonry and on giving of himself.

Brother Charles gives you vital information for running a successful lodge through step-by-step proven methods and even relates them to his own Blue Lodge based on his experience. It is my hope that the brethren who read this work will truly take it to heart and use what they've learned to "Best Work and Best Agree" for the benefit of all Masonry.

I'm deeply honored to have been asked to participate in this worthwhile and impressive endeavor. Thank you, Brother Charles Matulewicz, my friend and Brother.

Kenneth R. Taylor, Right Worshipful Grand Secretary
Grand Lodge of A.F. & A.M. of Maryland

Opening

This book is for the Brother who wants to pay something forward. My father always told me that when you borrow something, you should always return it better than you found it. So if I borrow an ax, I sharpen it… we as Masons have to realize that we are just passing through the fraternity and serve as stewards for those gentlemen who are going to be knocking on the preparation room door whom we have never met. For you I have compiled a guidebook in Anthropology, of leadership… of change management. You see Brother, It does not matter what degrees you have or what titles, or accolades you've accumulated. All that matters are Brotherly Love, Relief, and Truth. This book is a gift to you, and I am entrusting you with a task: make your Lodge better than it was when you entered through the preparation room door.

I am going to make a distinction between members of a Lodge and Masons in a Lodge. Being a member of the fraternity infers having a dues card while being a Mason isn't something to have rather it is something to practice. Masonry gives you tools to apply to moral situations and sadly you are not going to be able to do anything with these tools if you do not have someone teach you the practice of Masonry. Imagine that your only Masonic experience was the actual degrees… hey put this on, come this way… sit here, this guy is going to talk to you. After which the Worshipful Master expounds: Hey this stuff happened to you and get a load of these symbols for some reason. Having just experienced Masonry through the degree are you going to have any frame of reference to apply those moral lessons to the world through which you are moving? Probably not. I pose to you that you only learn to apply the lessons of Masonry by interacting with your Brothers. Masonry is an investment in the other, an investment in making moral choices such that a Brother may learn from the experience of his Brethren. The net outcome of which is the younger Brother is learning to apply the lessons of Masonry from his elder Brethren, they are investing in him so that with luck that young Mason never has to say, I wish I had known then what I know now. That only works If you engage all the Brethren, and you can only engage all the Brethren if you find a way to bring them together. Please do not let your zeal for the craft allow you to discount any Mason's practice. If you see yourself blaming those who came before you about the state of the Craft, consider that the old timers have devoted hundreds of hours on Masonry - they have been working to preserve the Lodge. **Why?** They did it for you.

Masonry is one of the few organizations where men come together and deploy Herculean efforts for men that they have never met yet. Your Masonic experience is dependent on the Masonic experience of your Brothers. Why would we focus on Culture instead of any number of other challenges that face the Craft? If the experience of going through the degrees is the mystical tie that unites all Masons, then the culture that develops in the Lodge over time is the cement that binds the Brothers. I think of a quote from Frank Herbert's Dune: "Parting with friends is a sadness. A place is only a place." The Temple is only a building, the Lodge is the assembled Brethren and I pose to you by putting Culture at the center of your Masonic experience planning you can create a continuity that isn't dependent on a progressive line or a gifted Worshipful Master, or even an engaging Grand Lodge. To stand the test of time strong culture gives strength in unity and provides a resilience to sustain the Lodge past any of our lifetimes.

This book is drafted around a series of questions; each one a start of a conversation on how you can make some progress in your Lodge. You will find it written in a conversational style and my opinions will tend to creep in, and for that I will apologize in advance. I want you to think about the Lodge. I don't really figure into this. Sit back and picture the officers and the sideliners thinking about those faces in the Lodge room over time. Men will shift through the officer chairs... new faces will appear on the sidelines and those old faces will fade away. Lodges change over time, but the collective efforts of those Brothers have created a culture that is as unique as the Brothers that make up the Lodge. And that culture endures. Every Mason's motivation to adopt Masonry is as integral to a working Lodge as your enthusiasm. This book is not a call to overthrow the old guard; this book is a set of tools that you can use to be a good steward of your Lodge, making it stronger than you found it. I believe you can do it, because I believe in Masonry, and I bel

A Visit to Lodge

Imagine you have gone to Lodge for the first time in years, and this meeting had the typical experience. You open, there are minutes, a younger Mason gives a short presentation on education, and you may have a degree. After the meeting, the Brethren are saying their goodbyes and some of the Brothers are talking in the banquet hall downstairs. You happen upon a conversation:

"I am having a hard time, work is so tough I haven't been to Lodge forever", said a Brother who appeared to be in his early thirties. "I understand," says a Brother who appears to be in his late sixties. The conversation continues talking about the news of the day and a few anecdotes about the Lodge… they laugh and talk about going to a pub to meet the rest of the guys after Lodge. "You know," says the older Brother. "You know the greatest regret that I ever had was that I spent all of those years climbing the corporate ladder and I missed so much. I missed birthdays and dinners. I missed recitals."

The older Brother sighs… "I think about it every time I see a first degree where they are explaining the 24-inch gauge. I spent all of that time working and shorted my family."

How old is your daughter? The older Brother says.

"She's almost two", says the younger Brother.

"Well, let me buy you a beer and then you have to get home, you only get so many of those years with your little one," said the older man.

That is Masonry… and that is the Masonic experience that I believe all men are looking for, it is that simple… and sadly there is nothing harder. We want to give Masonry away, and yet we do not have the words to enunciate the nature of this gentle Craft. It's a bitter irony that this organization that often

3

speaks of seeking further light seldom realizes that the fragile spark of Masonry is passed not via a grand program but rather through one Brother to another in countless quiet conversations.

If you are willing to do the work, you can make the fraternity better than you found it. I pose to you that at no time in Masonry's history have so few Masons owed so much to the legion of Brothers who have come before. If you can be the Mason that you needed when you were younger you can effectively become a living rule, you can make a material difference in the lives of your Brothers and through them the world. So maybe you are a new Master Mason who is looking to help the Lodge you just joined, maybe you are a new officer... or maybe you are a Senior Warden who is just realizing that you are going to be the ringmaster of this three-ring circus in a few short months. Whichever of these scenarios speak most to you, keep reading on.

One

How do I talk to someone about Masonry?

Talking about Masonry is the hardest thing for many Masons to do which may sound ridiculous. How is it possible that an organization which a man can spend hundreds if not thousands of hours working with is hard for him to describe when asked? I am going to go out on a limb and say it is because there are as many Masonries as there are Masons. Imagine going on a trip... perhaps to Europe. You see the architecture of Scandinavia with its natural woods and straight lines is distinctly different from the wide boulevards and tall windows of Paris. Those architecture elements are specific to their time and place. Imagining visiting some of the Lodges within an hour drive from your home. There may be a Lodge with Victorian ornaments, a Lodge that was built in the 1960's further in the suburbs that looks like a community center with wood paneling and a giant refreshment hall, and you may find a small-town Lodge above a country store. Each of these Lodges were built in a specific time and place and they all are going to have a culture as unique as their architecture. When you visit each of those Lodges where you ask the Brethren who call those Lodges home to talk about their Lodge each one will tell you a unique story: their memories and the stories that have become myths handed down Mason to Mason.

Why did you join the fraternity?

This is not a one word or even sentence length answer. This is not some off the cuff answer. This is a description of the first step of this Masonic journey that you started, and it is the most important story in Masonry: your Masonic story. Your story is the "why" that brought you to the Craft and keeps you engaged. This is what you are going to share with any person who asks about Masonry.

At some point someone is going to ask you "what is Masonry" and what are you going to say?

People respond to stories, so it is incumbent on you being able to tell your Masonic story to be able to provide a way for the inquirer to relate to Masonry. To effectively have the inquirer see themselves in Masonry. If you can share your "why" or the impetus that had you start your personal Masonic journey then the inquirer can see how you feel about the craft, and with luck they can see themselves in it as well. The best stories (or advertising) present itself to the viewer as a mirror that they can, for all intents and purposes, see the reflection of who they would aspire to be in. Your story, your why is the most powerful tool you have when talking to a potential new Mason.

So you are probably wondering now, how do I begin?

With the beginning of course. So let us do an exercise asking the question why?

I will get us started:

Q. Why did you become a Mason?

>A. I was looking for something to do.

Q. Why?

>A. All I was doing was going to work and coming home, my wife was working late at the time too. So I guess I was looking for some friends. After college I did not have many.

Q. Why?

>A. I suppose I was a little lonely, and I thought it might be something to do.

Q. So Why the Masons?

>A. My Grand Dad was a Mason, I always respected him and after he passed away some Masons performed a Memorial Service, I

hadn't thought about it for years and when driving through the next town over to get to the highway I saw a Masonic Lodge and started to think about the fraternity.

So the last reason allows us to tie all of the prior questions together.

Q. So why did you become a Mason:

> A. So my Grand Dad was a Mason and after he had passed there was a Masonic Memorial Service, the ceremony really impressed me. All I was doing was working and coming home, and my wife was busy with her career, and I realized after college I did not have many friends and I was looking for something. I had not thought about the Masons for years and when I was driving through town, I saw the sign for the Lodge, and something clicked. I called the Lodge and was sitting in the same seat that you are in now asking questions.

I want you to ask yourself the same thing. Ask yourself why you became a Mason five times… write the answers down and in the process, you are giving voice to the first act of your Masonic story. Like every story your Masonic story will have a past, present, and a future. Having captured why you joined we want to understand what keeps you coming back and be able to give that motivation a voice. When we talk to someone about Masonry, we want to tell them your Masonic Story which is going to consist of three parts: why you joined, why you stay, and how you are better for having been a Mason.

We can forgo repeating the same questions and answer exercise for the other two components: why you stay involved and how you have been made better for being in the craft. The concept is the same; you want to be able to clearly explain why you stay involved in Masonry and how Masonry has helped you be better than you were before you knocked on the preparation room door. So repeat those five why for the two questions:

1.) Why am I still involved in Masonry?

2.) How has Masonry made me a better man?

Let us look how the conversation would flow.

Q. Why did you become a Mason?

> A. "So my Grand Dad was a Mason and after he had passed there
> was a Masonic Memorial Service, the ceremony really impressed
> me. All I was doing was working and coming home, and my wife
> was busy with her career, and I realized after college I did not have
> many friends and I was looking for something. I had not thought
> about the Masons for years and when I was driving through town, I
> saw the sign for the Lodge, and something clicked. I called the
> Lodge and was sitting in the same seat that you're in now."

> "But I stay active because I enjoy the time with my Brothers. Over
> the years I have gotten really into the history and philosophy of the
> fraternity, and I like to be able to give that back to the Lodge."

Q. What did you get out of Freemasonry?

> A. "I think that I got way more out of being a Mason than I have
> ever spent doing Masonry. The fraternity invested in me. I am
> loud-shy, and I do not think I ever would have had the professional
> opportunities that I have had without the public speaking skills
> they helped me develop.

You want to be able to share these three pieces of your story because they
highlight a full spectrum of what can connect a man with Masonry. They
encapsulate what you are doing in Masonry (so he can see there is a path to
stay engaged) and finally how Masonry made you better.

So we went through those three components and asked ourselves five whys
for each component, what does that look like? Being able to tell your story is
way more compelling than either an elevator pitch or a series of facts about
the craft ever can be. People respond to stories and if someone asks them to

share your story and the authenticity will come through… and something real is something people want a part of. So, that begs the question: *what is your story*

Two

Someone wants to talk to me about Masonry, what now?

The inquiry scenario could unfold like this: You might receive an email inquiry to your Lodge website where a gentleman has written to the Lodge saying something to the effect, "I am looking to reach the lizard reptilian Illuminati, can your hidden masters contact me?" Let's ignore that one. Moving onto the second inquiry from the website we see a gentleman wrote saying: "I am looking for more information on Masonry, thanks - Charles."

Let's craft an Email reply.

We want to change the subject so that it cuts through their email noise (they have 7 million unread emails that you must be seen through). Pick a subject line that is not too salesy but creates some interest.

> EMAIL ONE: A scenario where the contact did not leave a call back number
>
> Subject: Hoping to help you with your questions about Freemasonry
>
>> Charles,
>>
>> Thank you for reaching out. There is so much information about Freemasonry online it can be hard to figure out where to begin. I am happy to answer your questions, tell you about the Lodge, and learn a little more about you. If there was a good number to reach you on, I can give you a call. What would be a good time to connect?
>>
>> Thanks,
>>
>> Charles Matulewicz
>>
>> 443.XXX.XXXX

We want to get our conversation out of the inquirer's inbox and get an opportunity to speak to them. We want to be able to make an actual connection with the person and get them into a conversation. People can blow off email so it's in our best interest to get this gentleman on the phone.

Think of your own inbox. There are likely thousands of emails in your inbox that you are never going to respond to. If it is not at the top of the pile it likely will never get responded to. Knowing how the inbox works you do not want your reply to a gentleman inquiring about Masonry to sink below the waterline.

Let us consider the second type of email, the email where someone left their number. CONGRATULATIONS – someone offering up their phone number is gold! If someone left their number, you want to take advantage of that and let's walk through how.

I want to make a confession; I use my caller ID to protect my time. If I do not recognize your number (and it does not look like a work-related call) I am going to let it go to voice-mail. If the person that you are calling back is under fifty, they are likely going to do the same thing, so it is incumbent on us to take advantage of the access that voicemail will provide. Voicemail will give you a captive audience, so it is best to prepare.

You want to make your voice-mail short and to the point: Who are you, why are you calling, what do you want, how can they reach you. You only get one first impression so planning out what you are going to say. So let's call back this second inquirer, a hypothetical Steve.

> Voice-mail follow-up

>> Steve, this is Charles from the local Masonic Lodge, I wanted to give you a call to answer your questions and see how I can help. Give me a call when you have a chance to talk 443.xxx.xxxx. Thank you.

We want to use the gentleman's first name, because let us be realistic… putting myself in Steve's shoes my last name is Matulewicz, what are the odds of the Masons pronouncing that correctly? We will identify ourselves as being with the local Masonic Lodge because they may not remember the specific name of the Lodge and at this point probably don't care, but they will remember the Masons. We do not want to mention membership right now instead we want to open the door to help the inquirer and be able to speak to them at length about Masonry.

EMAIL SCENARIO TWO: The Person included a phone number

> Subject: Charles Matulewicz – Called about your Freemasonry Inquiry
>
> Steve,
>
> Thank you for reaching out. There is so much information about Freemasonry online it can be hard to figure out where to begin. If you had a few minutes, I would be happy to answer your questions, tell you about the Lodge, and learn a little more about you. If there was a good number to reach you on, I can give you a call, what would be a good time to connect?
>
> Thanks,
>
> Charles Matulewicz
>
> 443.XXX.XXXX
>
> *notice we embedded our phone number in every email we want the person we are contacting to be able to contact us directly if they prefer and we are hoping to have our name and number recognizable enough not to send directly to voicemail when we do call.*

You want to be able to share your story with the inquirer. What you do not want to do is share the fact that some number of Presidents were Freemasons, that they can join this long list of appendant bodies. Let me ask you a question, have you ever been on a conference call that continues forever and think to yourself, "We could have just sent out an email for this and I am never going to get this hour of my life back?" You probably have, right? Nobody wants to be on a pointless call, and I am going to tell you why, because we all are acutely aware that the most precious resource that we have is time… and we can feel our time and attention being siphoned away throughout the business day. We have all been sitting at a table with a man who has expressed interest in the Fraternity, and someone begins explaining the York and Scottish Rites... please do not do that. A man inquiring about the Masons wants to hear about Blue Lodge Masonry. The one exception to this rule is if the man has been impacted by the Shriner's Hospitals. If he has a connection, I want you to say, "The Shriner's Hospitals are the world's greatest charity, and every Shriner is a Mason. Can you share your story about the Shriners?" And listen to the man's story. This is terribly similar to the question I am going to ask him if he shares that his Grandfather, Dad, friend, etcetera was a Mason. I just want you to ask him something to the effect of: "You mentioned a Masonic connection, how did your *Grandfather's* being a Mason make an impact on you? You can say something similar with the youth groups. If you are sitting across from a young man, who is juggling school part-time and working full time you are going to speak to them about why the Fraternity is valuable enough to dedicate their finite time to.

When in doubt consider this approach:

Tell your Story

 Ask them about themselves

Talk about what makes your Lodge unique

Discuss fit i.e. ask them why they were drawn to Masonry and candidly talk about what your Lodge does that is like the things that inspired them to contact the Lodge

call to action – Explain to them the petitioning process, what is involved in your jurisdiction, what the time commitment would be, and explain that if they want a petition, you will get them one.

So what does this activity look like in action?

Suppose we received an inquiry and we subsequently followed-up with a call... which in turn led us to a great conversation with the man inquiring about Freemasonry. Where do we go from here? We want to not only get to know him, we also want to understand his "why" or his impetus for considering the Craft. We want to talk through his motivations and why he is interested in Masonry. It is easy to become eager to share all that you know about Masonry and 'a beginning is a very delicate time'[1]. It is the beginning where the conversations are really all about the person who is on the other side of the proverbial table. We want to be able to understand the man inquiring, his motivation for inquiring, and what he is looking to achieve in Masonry.

Let's consider some practicalities about continuing the conversation.

Nobody likes a salesman (which hurts because I professionally ask people for money). Taking it to its root it may be the salesmen that we do not mind but rather the feeling that we are being sold that leaves a bad taste in our mouths. We can learn something from the process of selling. When you are participating in that art of selling it often takes dozens of attempts to connect with your prospects and sadly you are often only going to reach a small percentage of those prospects and turn a still smaller portion of them into sales. We are not selling something though, we are giving it away, so our approach is different. Think about that statement, we are not selling Masonry... we are giving it away. If in your conversation Masonry is not right for the inquirer that is fine, as timing is everything. Let me repeat that again, timing is everything. If the Craft is not a fit for the man today, there is no finessing the situation. Any convincing that you do on how it could work is simply convincing yourself which you likely will regret when you sell the man on the ease of Masonry and a year later the newly sold Brother fails to advance.

---

[1] Borrowed from Frank Herbert's Dune – Which is a great fiction book that captures politics, tradition, and zeal. Perfect for someone going through the officer line.

When I was speaking to candidates often timing was the problem. I always explained to them the full requirements of joining in my jurisdiction. Explaining the commitment of catechism (or whatever the specific requirements of your jurisdiction may be) is critical so the petitioner can understand if they have the number of hours required to commit to the process of becoming a Mason. You can give them the degrees, but you cannot change the length of their twenty-four-inch gauge. The refrain - *it is only a couple of hours a week* is one we do not want to mindlessly offer up because if our candidates hear it and it happens to not be the case you have set your Lodge up to fail to meet our candidates' expectations. Maybe the man takes care of an elderly parent, perhaps they are working two jobs to make ends meet, perhaps they never saw their Dad much… and he wants to be able to spend some time with his kids while they are young. The most important man in the fraternity is the man who is knocking upon the preparation room door, let us not make assumptions about his commitments outside of the Blue Lodge please. He may not be able to commit to the work because he has committed to other things. Don't lose heart but remember the concept of timing… Just because today is not a fit because of time does not mean tomorrow will not be. Maybe his children have gotten a little older or perhaps his job has changed. The inquiry that was made 48 months ago does not go bad like a truck full of bananas, on the contrary… circumstances may have changed, *if only someone reached out to them and reminded them about Masonry.* How many good Masons do we lose because we don't reach out to the man who inquired three years ago and never contacted us again because all he remembers is that the Lodge wasn't a good fit those thirty-six months ago?

The list of inquirers is going to be a resource that you can leverage again in the future. It is going to be something you can go back to again and again. I am going to recommend you take all your inquiries and put them in google docs on a list that can be referenced down the road. I mention google docs because you want to place that list where multiple people can get to it. When you have an open house, reach out to these fellows annually inviting them out to something. Maybe you friend them on Facebook and keep in touch that way, whatever best suits you... consider reaching out between Thanksgiving and Christmas. These two holidays often have families together and are periods where men are reflecting on the year past and they may be more receptive to your outreach. I am calling your attention to these old inquiries because there is going to come a period when nobody is contacting your Lodge about Masonry and that is ok; these things are cyclical. The list of old contacts will ensure that your Lodge membership people are not sitting in a dark room hitting the refresh button on the Lodge email account or bemoaning that nobody is interested in Masonry any longer. Lodges that save their contacts have saved for a rainy day.

What Masonry requires of its petitioners is important but the most important person in this conversation is the inquirer that is talking to us about the Masonry they are seeking. How do we prepare ourselves for the questions that they are going to ask? Topics are going to vary from what types of activities that your lodge participates into the history of your Lodge so be prepared for some high-level information on these topics. If the man inquiring is investing his time in asking the best thing that you can do is accurately portray your lodge. We do not want to sell the inquirer anything, no, we want to carefully map the realities of the lodge with what they are looking for. Let us say for example the gentleman voices an interest in social activities. What social activities are you putting on? Talk to your experience, what types of Lodge activities are you participating in? Why do you like them? Speaking to things that have been memorable or meaningful to you allows for a conversation that is authentic and flow. Further you can express real enthusiasm for things that resonate with you. When in doubt or when you have taken this dialog as far as it can go give him a copy of your trestle board and invite him to something. This would give the gentleman inquiring an opportunity to meet some other Brothers and get a feel for the Lodge. Ask them what they are interested in and if your Lodge does any of those things mention them. If your Lodge does not do the things the inquirer is interested in but there is a Brother in the Lodge who does do these things make an introduction. Use the entire palette of talents and interests in the Lodge to help this gentleman find resources that can help him address his why. This is a man who came looking to improve themselves in Masonry so do not hesitate to learn more about them. They are who it is all about after all.

What are your expectations of your petitioners?

In Maryland we investigate our petitioners in the form of a committee. They go out and ask the petitioner something. We vote based on the findings of the committee. The man who has been elected to receive the degrees of ancient craft Masonry has a basic requirement they must learn the work. Essentially, they must be able to recite their catechism to show that they are duly proficient. If they owe us the work, we owe them a full description about what we are asking of them. Walk them through the requirements of your jurisdiction's catechism and tell them how often you have meetings and how often you have other activities. This is a two-way street, not a soliloquy... you want to ask things of them. What is their interest in Masonry? Did they have a family connection to Freemasonry? Who are they? Remember you are looking to find a man who is worth investing in, who is worth making a Mason. In the back of your mind you need to consider that the officers of the Lodge have spent hundreds of hours memorizing the work, some of these Brothers have been maintaining and supporting the Lodge for half a century... is the man you are speaking to going to be able to benefit from your Lodge's Masonry? Is the man you are speaking to going to come to the Lodge and make it better than he found it? Is he the type of man who contributes? Let us continue the conversation with our hypothetical inquirer, shall we?

If you happen to discover that nights are not good for him because he is taking care of his kids or maybe he works on the night that you are having your meetings, consider what is best for him. If your Lodge schedule does not sync with his please consider letting him know if there is a Lodge nearby that would better fit with his schedule. Offer to get him the contact info for a Brother at the Lodge that better meets his needs and make an introduction because if your Lodge is not a fit for him ensuring that he finds a place in the fraternity makes Freemasonry stronger. Every Mason who is out in the world living his daily life and just being a Mason increases the probability that a Mason will inspire others to inquire about Masonry. Use your judgment on how you can help each man on their Masonic journey.

Consider inviting the inquirer to meet with one or two Brothers from your Lodge. This will give him a chance to meet some Brothers and see the Lodge itself. It also serves a secondary function; to see if this person is really interested. Put yourself in the inquirer's shoes for a moment... showing up is a big commitment so the least you can do is try to give them the best return on the time they are dedicating to come out to speak with you. Consider inviting them on a night when they are going to be the most important person in the room. Inviting them to a visit where you are conferring the third degree on five Brothers is not going to necessarily be a good experience as the inquirer may not receive the personal attention that they are looking for. Although there is nothing wrong with having him to the Lodge when the Brethren are already assembled, consider an impartial third location; maybe a Starbucks or a diner, maybe the pub you visit after Lodge if you are not going to be able to give the inquirer the attention that he deserves.

Here is a good litmus test, if you cannot introduce the inquirer to three Brothers and sit with him for at least 30 minutes to answer his questions you may want to rethink inviting the gentleman out to visit the Lodge on that particular night. So let us say you have Lodge this coming week. There is a program so there should be good attendance... but you think to yourself, oh my program is a visit by the Grand Line Officers. That may not be a good time to have an intimate question and answer period with an inquirer as everyone is going to be running around worrying about the GrandMaster. Objectively that might not be the optimal night to have the inquirer visit. If you want to utilize the Lodge for a meeting point, keep the group to a minimum and select a night where you are rehearsing or doing an activity where you can focus on the inquirer. You only get one chance to make a first impression so look for a way to meet with the inquirer in such a way that you can put them at ease and give them a chance to actually get to know the

Brothers. Let's treat the inquirer like he is the most important person in the fraternity, as if he was the Grand Master, and focus on him and how he can get a feel for the type of Lodge that you have and the types of Brothers in it.

Three

Why do you want more members?

This question may not make any sense at first, of course we want more members! But let us get to the why of this question. Masonry has given me tremendous opportunities… I have spoken on Masonic topics all over my home jurisdiction and as I traveled all over my home state of Maryland some of the most interesting meetings happen after the Lodge meeting. This is where I discovered that one of the most frequent topics of conversation is, "hey Brother Charles, esoterica is nice, but how do we get more members?" This is where I came up with the maddening question: "Why do you want more members?"

There is nothing that will have your Brothers looking at you as if you were crazed faster than asking them sincerely, "Why do you want more members?"

Look if you are looking for more members to perform the basic function of the Lodge like filling officer chairs and filling committees than you are candidly outsourcing your Lodge's problems to your candidates. Does that sound fair?

What's the first rule of Blue Lodge?

Make Masons

What's the second rule of Blue Lodge?

Make Masons!

Make Masons and the membership problems will take care of themselves. That sounds like a banal platitude, but it is not. Modern Masonry in many places sadly reduces the Masonic experience to caveat emptor, or let the buyer beware. We make the petitioner solely responsible for understanding the quality and suitability of what they are joining before they petition and then when they find that their expectations and their real experience are so far apart that they wash out… and we subsequently say the candidate wasn't dedicated enough. We say that society has changed. We evoke any number of other excuses. The truth is we reduced Masonry to membership and the world does not need members, the world needs Masons. The world needs men who will stand by their word. Men who can have a conversation with someone of a different political bent and disagree as gentlemen and come together as Brothers. The world needs men who struggle to do the right thing but try anyway not looking who sees them do it. The world needs Masons.

So back to the problem at hand. The man we are speaking to has asked what Masonry is and we talked to him about our Masonic story, why we joined, why we stay involved in Masonry, and how it improved us for a specific reason… when the gentleman asks or infers what they can get out of Masonry we have to have a reply. It is not an unexpected question, and it is not one that is altogether inappropriate or one that signals mercenary motives. We are going to ask something of the petitioner, and it is only right that we can enunciate the true value of Masonry so share your story.

So if the world needs Masons, how do we get them? Before we proceed, I am going to ask you to consider this: The Grand Lodge prints dues cards, the Blue Lodge makes Masons. The Blue Lodge is where Masons get made and it is up to you to decide if you are willing to put in the work to make Masons. If you are committed, I am as well… so let's move on. We figured out a method for speaking to men and for following up with them when they are interested. Let us talk about what we have to work with.

Four

What are we working with here?

I want you to assemble a list of your members, including their ages, and where they live and put it in an excel spreadsheet. This will require you to be exceptionally nice to the secretary to obtain the data for all of this analysis, so be nice and thank him for the work that he does because there are few jobs more thankless. *You know that one of the few jobs you are guaranteed for life once you get it is being the Secretary of a Masonic Lodge?* But enough fun, back to work. Go online and find the average life expectancy for men in the US (at the time of this writing it is ~78.54 years). This is going to be slightly morbid, be prepared. What is the average age of your Lodge… probably around 62-67 years young? Sort that spreadsheet by the age column and I want you to count the number of your Brothers who are over the average life expectancy age, write that number down. What proportion of your men are at or over the average life expectancy? Add up all the ages, what is the average age… let's write that number down as well. You are never going to be able to stop men being called from labor, but you need to know where the Lodge is really sitting in terms of its member rolls.

Let us segue into the concept of 2B1ASK1. You may have seen this appear on bumper stickers, or one of the elder brethren may have brought this up when speaking about membership. First let me admit that this is not a bad concept… the problem is that it has reached a point of diminishing returns. Let me explain. There was a time when everyone was a Mason and those who were not Masons were likely Moose, Elk, or Knights of Columbus. That period in which the density of men belonging to fraternal orders was high meant you were likely going to have a Mason in your social circle somewhere. Such is no longer the case. These days if the average age of membership is pushed into retirement and membership is significantly off peak what are the odds that you are going to know a Mason to even ask if you are forty or younger? What are the odds that you are going to even know what a Mason is? I have a story about this very thing, my neighborhood consists mainly of younger professionals and one of my neighbors struck up a conversation with my wife about the logos on the back of my car (yes, I succumbed to that Masonic temptation). My spouse was asked what those logos are, and my wife says, "oh Charles is a Mason". To which my neighbor replies something to the effect that with all these old stone homes he must get a great deal of work. She just had no idea what Masons were outside of the operative kind... I was the only one that she knew. The 2B1ASK1 program worked when there was a high density of Masons, but once we lose that critical mass, we are no longer able to capitalize on our network of connections for members. That is a long-term problem and one that you will find endemic across Lodges and Grand Lodges throughout the country. If those days are gone, we can opt to either play offense or play defense... So let's not mourn the past but look to build a Lodge for another century. To do that we need to understand what we have to work with.

Consider the half-life of your Lodge, or the timeframe in which your roll of members will decrease 50%. You now have a spreadsheet containing the members and their ages and we have calculated the average age. Now let us add a column and subtract their ages from that 78-year life expectancy. You can calculate the number of Brothers you are going to lose over the next 10 years. How many Brothers are you going to need to bring in to keep your Lodge at a stable number of members? Let's say that I have 60 men that I am going to have called from labor over the next decade, that's a scary number but that means that I am going to need to bring in 6 guys each year for the next 10 years in order to hold my membership at its present levels. That is a problem, but a much more manageable problem than bringing in 60 guys all at once.

By estimating how many of our Brethren are being called from labor within a set period we can determine our replacement rate, but the problem is more complex. Look at the number of Brothers who have come in over the past several years, what's the difference? Let us say we brought in 40 guys in the past decade, we are on our way to that sixty number to keep our membership in equilibrium. The problem we are going to have with this cohort of 40 Brothers is that they likely joined the fraternity in order to make friends, if they had a slew of friends outside the fraternity, they likely would not have joined in the first place. How many of these Brothers are still active? How many Brothers are bringing lost to non-payment of dues? That is a hole in the bucket and something that you can directly impact. So let us look through those numbers. You may need to ask your Secretary for more information you are going to need to pull this data together. Be nice when you ask Brother Secretary for help... he does not have an easy job.

There is an interesting question that I want you to consider while you are looking at the membership: what percentage of the Brothers still live in the state? It is great to have hundreds of members but knowing how many are actually in the area is going to be key later when we try to determine who we can reach out to for help within the Lodge and who we can reach out to in order to see if we can get them to come out to Masonic activities. Write down the number in state/out of state and keep it handy.

Knowing where you are with your membership numbers will show you how many Brothers are going to be called from labor and how many you are going to need to acquire in order to ensure that you are able to continue as a working Lodge. This is not a numbers game and I am not trying to conflate members with Masons, but you are going to need to understand who can help you with the work of the Lodge and also what your year over year revenues are going to be so that you can plan for all of the fun that you are going to have.

Five

Who are the Brothers in the room?

The cruelest thing we can do is to put someone into a situation in which they are not going to be successful. We do not want to have a man inquire and move him through the degrees only to raise him to the sublime degree of Master Mason and hand him a ritual book and a staff (unless of course that this is the Brother's why). Consider what infrastructure that you have in terms of the Brothers who are in the Lodge and available to support the activities of your Lodge.

Do you have a sign in book set-up in the Tyler's room? I want you to grab it and if you have a chance also take the sign-in book that preceded it. We want to look at the people who have signed in over the past decade. Let us break down the names in the following categories:

a. Regular attendees (writing the years they were regularly attending)
b. Brothers attending 2-3 Meetings a year (writing the years of the meetings)
c. Annual attendees 1 meeting a year (writing the years of the meetings)

Look at your visitors as well, are there Brothers who are coming to your meetings at regular intervals?

- Regular visitors (writing the years of the meetings)

Now that you have those categories listed, write down the names of the Brothers under the appropriate category. We want to parse the Masons who were filling the seats and understand what types of attendees that you are seeing at meetings.

Were you able to grab the attendance book? Perfect! Flip through the pages of the book and see what the average number of attendees are. Take a year of meetings, add the total attendees up (don't forget to include the officers) and divide the total sum by the total number of meetings that you had during the year. Let's do the same thing for a decade's worth of meetings. Anecdotally I have found that you typically only get 10-15% of your members out to any given meeting across Maryland. Traveling throughout my jurisdiction that rule has held firm, what is your average number? How has that changed annually?

Are there meetings that had Brothers packing the place? Was there a year when the attendance was up? Are there meetings where there were an abnormally high number of visitors? This is all great information. Write the dates for these strange meetings. This list is what you are going to use to reach out to some of the Past Masters.

We are looking at the attendance for the past decade, asking the secretary for a list of the phone numbers for the past decades' worth of Worshipful Masters and their years in the East. Let us call each of them starting with the most recent and working our way backwards. Ask them about their year in the East and to share some of their memories, then let us work on some questions.

- If there are meetings which have a remarkably high attendance let us ask the Past Master about it.
  - a. "PM Matulewicz, there was a great attendance for the September 15, 2014 meeting, what was the program for the evening?"
- If the average attendance of one year was higher than others... ask about it.
  - a. "The second half of 2014's attendance was really high, what was happening at the lodge then?"

If there are any other patterns that you can see from the sign-in book let us, ask the Past Masters. They are going to want to share things with you, all you must do is ask. Towards the end of the conversation ask them if we can share some names with them to see if they remember the Brothers who were attendees or visitors. Read the highlights of the categories of attendees to the Past Master and see what feedback they can provide. Begin the process with the most recent Past Masters working backwards. I say work backwards because the most recent Past Masters are likely going to be able to potentially introduce you to the attendees and contributors. Sadly the odds for a warm introduction will decrease the further we go back in time. Looking back to the conversations about your Lodge attendees we can use the last year that the Brother was in Lodge… for example say PM Matulewicz was in the East in 2014 if you see there was a Brother who was actively coming to Lodge in 2014, but then fell off at the beginning of 2015 ask the Past Master if he knows him. If he does know, ask him if there is any information that he can share. You may be able to gain insight into who this Brother who attended things and then fell off the earth.

We want to be able to glean any information that we can about those Brothers who had been attending. Who were their friends? Why did they join? What did they like about Masonry? What were they involved in at the Lodge… those types of questions will give you a feel for who these Brothers are and what their reason for being part of your lodge is?

While you have the Past Masters on the phone there is one last piece of data that you want to get. Get a feel for ritualists who did not advance to the Oriental chair. Look, we ask a great deal of the men who are preparing to lead our Lodges. In Maryland they need to be a ritualist, a manager, and a leader – THAT IS A BIG ASK. With more and more demands placed on men professionally and personally the bandwidth to make it all the way through those chairs is harder and harder so there may be resources that you do not see in Lodge often. There may be Brothers who went through the chairs to a point and then did not make it to the East for one reason or another. These Brothers were committed enough to the Lodge to progress to a point any may be resources that you can tap later for assistance as you are looking to improve your Lodge experience. While you are asking those Past Masters about the Lodge in their years realize that they were stewards of the Lodge. All of those hours dedicated to moving the Lodge towards the future makes those Past Masters a great resource for you. They have a vested interest in the success of the Lodge so don't hesitate to leverage them (let's cover how we can specifically speak to Past Masters a little later).

Having gotten to know some of the Past Masters and asked for their feedback... and having pulled together a listing of who has been attending. We are going to use those lists in a little bit. Let us look at one of the elephants in every Lodge room: travel time.

Six

What is the elephant in the room when it comes to Lodge attendance?

Typically when we have programs that are not well attended, we attribute the attendance to low interest, but what if we reframed the way we think about attendance? We as Masons do not give a great deal of consideration to the commute time most people deal with daily. We drive to work, and we drive home, and this is an externality that you need to consider when we think about the Lodge. Time is the most valuable resource we all have… that is probably the reason that we talk to those youngest entered apprentices about dividing your time via the symbol of the 24-inch gauge. What's your metro area's average commute time? Here in the greater Washington-Baltimore metro area we average a ~32-minute commute time each way. Why do I bring this up? This is the elephant in the room that we need to consider.

Let us say you have a Brother at your Lodge, and he is really, really enthusiastic. Even he has a business problem in the back of his mind each time he comes to Lodge. Even this enthusiastic Brother asks himself if this meeting is worth adding another 'x' minutes to his day. In my jurisdiction I have found that there are two cohorts of guys in the room a) the retirees and b) the working Brothers. Put all of the Past Masters to the side in this discussion as they have a vested interest in the Lodge, so they are more prone to drive farther to attend (*Stockholm syndrome*) … set to looking at the two groups: how far are they residing from the Lodge? My findings have a threshold of fifteen minutes of additional drive time each way. Meaning the guys who are attending have a fifteen-minute drive to/from or a max total of thirty minutes round trip to get to Lodge. Traveling around Maryland I have found very few working Brothers who are living further than fifteen minutes away from Lodge are regularly attending. When speaking to the Brothers at other Lodge's this seems to be the case throughout the metro area. What does that mean to you? Well, you have to create a compelling reason to head to an activity or your Lodge meeting because at the end of the day just getting to the Lodge is not a quick fifteen-minute drive. You have to widen your gaze for the working

Brother. It's a cumulative process: ~1 hour and 4 minutes of windshield time, plus putting on a jacket and tie, plus the minutes, plus… plus… plus. You need to be able to provide a compelling reason to get behind that wheel.

For our exercise Google the average commute time for your metro area and write that number down. Look at the membership list, place the Brothers who are out of state to the side and just look at just those Brothers we are in your state. If you can get their zip codes we can calculate the travel time for them (I'll throw a link here for a website that can help: https://www.zip-codes.com/distance_calculator.asp). Go back to our lists of frequent attendees and highlight those members that are coming to Lodge. Add their drive times together? What is the transit time there? Average them together to come out with the average transit time, or 'x'.

What percentage of your membership is within 'x' minutes?

Putting the population of Brothers who are out of state and the Past Master's to the side, the total number of Brothers who are within the average drive time are a tremendous resource. Once you have had your conversations with the Past Masters you are going to have information on what has been happening in past years, what was successful, and with any luck you will also get some detail on the Brothers who were attending things and then stopped. It is time to look at how we are going to reach out to those Brothers who are members of your Lodge. If we understand what Brothers are within a reasonable drive to Lodge, we can see whom we can ask for assistance.

Seven

What do we do about the Brothers who are out of state?

How often do you speak to the Brothers from out of state? You know, those names on your rolls that may not have been to Lodge in years? As the average age of your Lodge likely is going to skew older you are going to see Brothers tending to move during retirement either for tax reasons or maybe to be closer to their children and grandchildren. Subsequently as the proportion of the out of state membership grows larger there is a real risk of Brothers just opting to not pay their dues. But this is not just about the dues, we do not want the Brothers who are far away to feel forgotten.

Does your Lodge send out a trestle board that communicates meeting details to your membership? If you do let me, ask you this: does sending this out alone create enough of an incentive to maintain the connection to your Lodge for the Brother? Consider doing something to create a more personal connection to the Lodge for the Brothers who are far away. You do not want a member of your Lodge to fade into the background and just fall off the radar, so it is worth doing something special for these members of your Lodge.

Consider writing a letter to those out of state Brothers sharing what is going on in the Lodge. Share a little detail on the Brothers who are joining or how you feel the Lodge is faring. You want to create a connection to the Lodge and let these Brothers know that they are not forgotten for two reasons. One, it is the right thing to do. And two you do not want to start hemorrhaging members who no longer see the value of maintaining their membership in your Lodge; it's bad for cashflow. Imagine being out of state yourself. How would it feel to get something from your Brothers that is not a dues bill or a list of meetings that you cannot attend?

Example outreach letter:

May 4th, 2014

Brethren,

This is the halfway point of the Masonic year, and we have a great deal to yet accomplish. The Brothers of Palestine have been raising Master Masons and coordinating educational activities... and it now looks like the long stretch of EA degrees is approaching. Your open house was quite a success, and we are looking at six petitions to vote on and an additional four more in the wings. The officers will be initiating a group of men who are interested and looking for just what we have to offer a safe harbor in the modern world, where the wicked cease from troubling, and the weary shall find rest.

On the 8th we plan on having a Masonic Bling night or rather a "Show and tell night" I would ask all of the Brethren so inclined to bring a Masonic memento to the meeting and share a little about what it is and what it means to them. I think it will be a bit fun and a nice break from degree work and education.

The Lodge has been active and is looking forward to a docket of social activities:

> The Ladies and significant others of Palestine Lodge are doing a lady's night out on 5-15-14 in old Ellicott City.

> We will be having a cigar night at 2:00 5-24-14 at slow burns on Main Street in Catonsville.

> Our Baseball game is taking place on 6-14-14; please see Brother Robby for tickets.

> We are still coordinating our Family picnic, our visit to Black Ankle Vineyards, as well as our Ladies night. Please stay tuned.

> Brother SW will be exemplifying the second degree the night of 5-15. He and his line of officers have been working hard to sharpen their skills. I hope that you will be able to come out to support him as he moves towards completing his qualifications to sit in the East, if so elected.

Many of our Brothers are not able to get out to Lodge; and given the opportunity I would like to share with you what has been going on at your Lodge. Brother CJ and his wife Angie had a boy, Jacob

Thomas... Angie and the little man are doing well. Brother Charlie is doing well, after his fall he had limited mobility and was unable to attend Lodge. We plan on installing him during our 5-8-14 meeting. Brother Joe, whose computer died, presented to the Lodge a program on the idea of mystery schools and Greek mythology... he and Brother Stone had a short debate on the idea that Masonry had more to do with Egypt than perhaps the Ancient Greeks. The Brothers poked fun at Brother Leidy, and a good night was had by all.

One of the unique privileges of being the Master is to assist with the presentation of service awards. We presented three 50 year awards at the last meeting of the month of April and had a packed house. Brothers G., H., and PM F. were in attendance and the Grand Inspector presented awards on behalf of the Grand Master. What an honor it was to support those Brothers who have supported the Lodge for so many years!

One of the activities that was a bit different in the 2014 year was that we have made a special effort to reach out to our widows. This has involved me writing letters to each of them and will continue with our presentation of holiday cards this year as well as a holiday party for all the Brethren where they are our special guest. We will publish more as we come closer to the holiday season. We plan on continuing meetings through June to accommodate our degree work.

I will keep you abreast of the goings on of the Lodge, and in my thoughts and Prayers. Being Master was so much fun in 2013 I wanted to thank you for letting me try it again this year... What an exciting time to be a member of Palestine Lodge.

Sincerely and Fraternally,

Charles

I wrote letters to my out of state Brothers and mailed them in the same envelope as the Lodge Trestle board to hold down the cost. Maybe you do not have the bandwidth to write a letter or have done away with mailings altogether. Consider some alternative outreach ideas:

- Divide the list of out of state Brothers amongst some of the officers and give them a call to check in on them.
- Send a regular email out to the out of state Brothers such as:

- o   Asking them to share a memory of the Lodge
- o   Ask them what they would like to see the Lodge do more of
- o   Ask them if they have any advice for you
- o   Share some biographical information on the newest members or the officers
- o   Ask them to talk about Masonry with a friend or family member.
- o   Offer to find them a local Lodge to attend if they so desire.

You have the power of the pen so think of your Lodge and its culture. Consider doing something that would make the Brother you are contacting feel special and reach out to that cohort of Brothers who are out of state in order to ensure that they don't feel forgotten. Making them feel remembered will encourage them to talk about Masonry to their families and likely encourage them to remember sending in their dues for the next fiscal year.

Eight

What is my Lodge culture?

The Lodge experience is owned by multiple generations and too much change can make some of your Brothers feel alienated or unvalued so as you plan you want to carefully consider the culture of the Lodge. Culture is a soft word, but it is the glue that holds your merry band of Brothers together. It is the shared experience of your Lodge. Think back to your own Lodge experience. How are the Brothers and visitors greeted when they come into the Lodge... how do the Brothers interact when they are having a meal together? Consider the fraternal aspect of your Lodge. Where does the Lodge have its after Lodge experience? How do the Brothers say their goodbyes? Consider all these variables together and see how they impact the experience of the man coming in the door. This may not be an easy exercise for you. But you can frame it another way.

Think of Lodge culture as that cement which unites Masons together in their Lodge as a society of friends and Brothers.

Looking back at those conversations that you had with your Past Masters, what were the common themes? As the Past Masters talked about that year in the Oriental chair, what were the commonalities between the stories that they tell? Between the stories of the Past Masters and your own reflections on your fraternal experience you are starting to get a picture of the culture of your unique Lodge.

Wrap your mind around this idea, as it is central to the vision of Masonry that I believe critical for the Mason in the twenty-first century to adopt the philosophy: *there are as many versions of Freemasonry as there are Masons.* By extension, there are as many Lodges as there are versions of Masonry. There are charity Lodges... There are fraternal experience Lodges, there are ritual Lodges, etcetera. The themes are as varied as the architecture of the Temples in which they practice their craft. What if you visited a neighboring

Lodge tomorrow? If you asked a sample of Brothers to describe their Lodge, you may get themes from across the spectrum:

- We really focus on the ritual at my Lodge.
- My Lodge is like home, we always make a point to greet every brother.
- I do not think I have ever felt alone since I joined the Lodge, and the meetings after the meetings are always a way to enjoy the company of the Brethren.
- There is always something that the Brothers are looking to teach me at Lodge.

Maybe one theme that you were expecting does not appear often in the conversation – *THAT IS OK*! If that missing theme is your 'why' for being involved in the Craft, you want to be careful as its natural to suffer confirmation bias[2]. You could fall into a trap where you see the Masonry being practiced by your neighboring Brothers as something less because it is not a mirror image of your Lodge. Masonry reflects a specific time and place. The Masonry you were looking for when you knocked on the west gate may not necessarily be the Masonry that the men who conferred the degrees on you thought they were conferring. Since the ritual imparts its lessons via symbol and allegory, and it is the receiver who ultimately gives those symbols meaning, we never really confer two of the same degrees no matter how letter perfect the work. The four hypothetical themes spelled out by the bulleted list above suggest that you have visited a Lodge that is serious in its ritual, warm, and big on fellowship, and seems to be investing in the development of the Brethren. Since a Lodge is greater than its component parts and you have seen some broad themes, you want to remember that you are 1 of a number of Brethren. If you want to improve their Masonic experience, you don't want to lose sight of the fact that it isn't your Lodge; it's a common space for all of its members. Since we have many cohorts of Brothers working in the Lodge, we

---

[2] Confirmation bias - The tendency to search for, interpret, focus on, and remember information in a way that confirms one's preconceptions.

want to garner representative data from all of them in order to improve the Lodge experience for not only them, but also the man who has not yet knocked on the preparation room door. So let's ask your Brothers what they wanted when they were in the preparation room and what keeps them engaged today and see what their stories tell us.

Ask

Ask, and it shall be given you; seek, and ye shall find; knock, and it shall be opened unto you

Matthew 7:7

We need to ask the Brethren as they have all the answers that we need. No program could be simpler and ironically no plan could be harder: ask. First, we are going to revisit the lists that we compiled earlier. We are now going to reach out to the men within the average commute time that never come to Lodge. Following up after with every Brother who was a regular attendee in the past decade. That sounds daunting however we are breaking the problem into smaller parts to make it more manageable.

We can approach this problem by using e-mail and creating a survey. First start with the survey's purpose as in what are we looking to understand? I would posit that we want to capture the 'why' of those Brothers: why they joined, why they are active, what they want to do. Once acquired you can take this data and plot out the activities that you want to engage the membership with. No one wants to throw a party which nobody shows up to, so it behooves us to understand what Brothers want to do.

There are several platforms which are low cost or optimally no cost that can help facilitate the survey. Platforms such as SurveyMonkey or Google forms can be leveraged to create your survey. The most cost effective/feature rich platform you can utilize would be using google forms. Google forms is a flexible platform that will support you in designing your own survey. There are pre-build modules, and you can send the form directly to the Brethren from the form itself and later tabulate the results. Remember to always place email addresses in the blind carbon copy (BCC) field. Some of your Brethren may not want to share their emails with the world (and check your jurisdiction's rules in order to ensure compliance).

Let's proceed by collecting the e-mail addresses for the three cohorts:

> Cohort A – Brothers within the average transit time to the Lodge who do not come

> Cohort B – Brothers who have attended Lodge regularly in the past decade

> Cohort C – Past Masters

We are splitting the groups apart because we want to know more in particular about the Brothers who could make a reasonable commute to Lodge activities but do not. This survey will give us a chance to see the Lodge through their eyes and give us an opening to engage them to see if we can invite them to come out to some activities tailored specifically to them. We are breaking out the Past Masters because we do want their insights, but we want to be able to look at them as a separate community because they are generally all in on your Lodge. The Past Masters are likely going to come back to the Lodge repeatedly and be active (likely there is going to be minimal convincing to get them to a Lodge activity as they are vested in the Lodge's success).

Your goal is to get responses to your survey so it would behoove you to send out a warm email to get the audiences engaged. Draft up a quick three-line email explaining that you are working on a project for the lodge and that you need the recipient's help. Taking the time to explain why the recipient should fill out your questions will help increase your feedback.

Having informed the Lodge that you are sending out a survey it is time to consider what you want to know. In the process of designing your questions you will want to understand why men came to the fraternity and what they are expecting now that they are in it. Consider these questions as starting points:

- Why did you join the Lodge?
- Are you active in the Lodge?
    - If you are active, why?
- If you do not make it to Lodge, why?
- What would make Lodge more interesting?
- What could make the Lodge more welcoming?
- Is Masonic Education interesting to you?
- Are social events interesting to you?
- Are family events interesting to you?
- Is degree work interesting to you?
- What is the purpose of Freemasonry?
    - Does our Lodge meet your expectations for that purpose?

You can amend as needed however the questions were conceptualized to get as holistic a view as to what the Lodge is interested in and what they want in as few questions as possible. If you do change the questions paint with a wide brush. Be careful in your wording as you do not want to get too into the weeds into specifics at this point remember that you can always follow-up with respondents individually after you receive their submission. As a matter of course you do want to set up your survey so you can identify an individual Brother's responses as you want to be able to put respondents in buckets so you can invite them to activities that resonate with them. Imagine you have an idea for a family picnic. If you have already identified that a section of the Brethren who don't regularly attend Lodge activities but are interested in family events, you have a group of people you can reach out to personally to invite the activity. You can continue to do this thematically for every type of activity that you may be interested in coordinating. I have included sample questions as an addendum at the end of the text for your use.

May I digress for a minute? I want to talk about why we need to ask the Brethren what they want as opposed to just plowing ahead with an amazing program? We need to bring the Brothers together because it is through that togetherness that the lessons of the craft are learned. Just receiving those degrees does not mean that you know what to do with those symbols and allegories when the situation calling for their use arises. You need someone to show you how to use those Masonic tools. Ancient Craft Masonry, like its operative counterpart, is the same way: Masons need to be shown how to practice their craft by those men who walked the path before them. It's a Joseph Campbell[3] moment:

> We have not even to risk the adventure alone
>
> for the heroes of all time have gone before us.
>
> The labyrinth is thoroughly known ...
>
> we have only to follow the thread of the hero path.
>
> Joseph *Campbell*

The Master did his part in making you aware of our working tools by calling your attention to their proper application. But it is the craftsman who labor alongside you in the world who teach you when to apply those symbolic tools by sharing their experiences. This is why activities that bring the Brothers together are so important, why engaging the Brothers is so important because if our Lodges are only conferring degrees, we are sending workmen into the world and hoping that they apply the gifts that our system has conferred upon them. Hope is not an effective strategy. But enough pontification... let's get back to our survey (hopefully agreeing that our Masonic experience is fulfilled through the Masonic experience of others).

---

[3] Joseph Campbell: was an American professor of literature at Sarah Lawrence College who worked in comparative mythology and comparative religion. His work covers many aspects of the human experience. His text: Hero with a Thousand Faces was formative for George Lucas's writing of Star Wars and an interesting text on Mythology for any Mason.

Having put our questions together we now have our Survey ready for dissemination; we have our three cohorts, and we are ready to start emailing some Brothers. First and foremost do you have emails for all the Brothers? When we sent out this survey, we wanted to not send out individual emails please use the blind carbon copy field (BCC). We want to blind carbon copy because we do not want to inadvertently share a Brothers email with everyone else and because nobody wants to have hundreds of *replies to all* emails in their inbox. We want to make it easy and non-intrusive for the Brothers to participate. Please use Blind Carbon Copy… BCC is your friend, and it is going to make your life much easier.

Start out with the prep email. We want to prime the pump and ask the Brother receiving the email for help. We want to encourage them to reply and through that engagement open the door to future conversations about working with us as we plan wildly engaging things for the Lodge in the future.

An initial email could look like:

remembering to BCC: everyone to preserve their anonymity.

> Subject: Palestine Masonic Lodge: I need your help
> Brother,
>
> I hope that you are well. We are working on activities for the 2020 Masonic Year, and I need your help in planning. Over the next few days I will be sending out a short survey asking for your thoughts, I hope that you will be able to participate.
>
> Thank you, and if there is any help I can provide do not hesitate to reach out.
>
> Fraternally,
>
> Charles

Consider sending a variation of the above to the Brothers who participate and the Past Masters. The Brothers who have not attended Lodge may need some additional attention. They are not coming to Lodge activities for some reason, and they may need some additional attention to garner a response. Take a moment and consider the men in your Lodge, there are as many reasons for them to have joined and stayed active as there are Masons. Please don't conflate attending Lodge with being a good Mason. There are many reasons that keep men away from their Lodges. It wouldn't be fair for us to suppose they are somehow lesser Brothers because their Masonry does not have them working with you at the Lodge. Family or business may have kept them away, but children grow, and work situations change… and at a point it may be just inertia that keeps them away. How many people join a gym and go with gusto for a period only to have their workout regimen interrupted and their enthusiasm dampened? People who join gyms tend to not go back after their initial excitement and often it is not because they are not interested in building an Adonis-like physique but because they got out of a routine. Your outreach may be just the thing necessary to reengage a Brother who still finds meaning in Masonry but whose routine did not allow activity in the past.

An email to the Brothers who do not come to Lodge activities could look like:

> Subject: Checking in on you Brother
>
> Brother,
>
> We had not heard from you in a while and frankly we should have asked long ago. I am working on a project to reach out to all the Brothers to check in and I hope that you and your family are well. If there is any news that you can share or any help the Lodge can provide, please do not hesitate to reach out to me.
>
> Fraternally,
>
> Charles

The above is a quick introduction to reopen the communication and get yourself on the Brother's radar. We can follow-up with a second email with a call to action where we share what we are hoping to do and ask for their help:

Subject: Brother Charles checking in

Brother,

May I ask you for your help? I am working on activities for the 2020 Masonic Year, and I could use your help in planning. Over the next few days I will be sending out a short survey asking for your thoughts, I hope that you will be able to participate.

Thank you, and if there is any help I can provide do not hesitate to reach out.

Fraternally,

Charles

Why send two emails? Look, people generally like to help the eager upstart who is trying to make things better, but their inboxes are filled… so you need a way to get their attention. The Brother that you may be reaching out to may have a sour taste in their mouth from something that happened at the Lodge, or they may have stopped engaging because they no longer know any Brothers at the Lodge. You are setting the stage that you want to help them, and you want to help the Lodge. Most importantly you are setting a tone that they are needed, which is a feeling that is rarer and rarer these days. Setting the text as coming from you in the form of 'I' gives it a level or personalization and sets a tone that even if they haven't heard from the Lodge for a while here is a Brother who cares about me. While you may think it a salesy approach let me ask you this, shouldn't we know how all our Brothers in the Lodge are?

Having prepped the audience for the survey let's prepare our email to transmit the survey:

Subject: Brother Charles – Survey about the Lodge

Brother,

I hope that you will take a moment and fill out the survey I am working on to plan out 2020. Please click here: LINK TO SURVEY.

As always if there is anything that we can help with please let me know.

Fraternally,

Charles

Include a link within the body of the email as attachments may be filtered out by a Brother's email platform. Make the emails and correspondence your own, make it come through in your own voice (I actually talk like this… so my writing is true to life). Take these templates as starting points and craft them so they sound like they are actually coming from you.

We are going to start seeing responses come in over the next couple of days… give it two to three weeks to collect all of the answers. If you are using Google forms, you can export the responses directly to a .pdf and I would encourage you to save the data and share it with the officers. Later when you can clean up the data it would be worth sharing it with the entire population of your Lodge Brothers. Take a good look at the answers that you got back, there are going to be some that are surprising. What themes are arising?

Nine

How do I interpret this Data?

More is better. More lapel pins, more degrees, and of all the above all more data! The higher a response rate that you receive to your survey the more the feedback will reflect the total population of your Lodge. You may feel compelled to shoot for a 100% response rate, but do not worry, for an internally facing survey a 30-40% response rate is outstanding. With the right outreach to warm up your audience you should be able to achieve that between 40-50%. We broke the survey into several component parts: Why you joined, what you like, what they seem the Lodge lacking... All of this is vital information for understanding the motivations of the Brethren.

The survey is going to help you reflect on and refine those themes of your Lodge that your conversations with the Past Masters helped uncover. Since we sent out the survey in three cohorts let's start with the Past Master's feedback. Does the data reflect the answers from the limited population of Brothers that you had already spoken to? Are you seeing the same things as you heard from the calls that you have made already? What additional insights were you able to glean?

Let's conduct a thought experiment. Imagine we have received our surveys back. Look at the hypothetical feedback that we have received... directing your attention to the reasons why your Brothers joined. Look across the three cohorts and in your mind's, eye see that 20% of the Brothers who are active in the Lodge say that they joined because they wanted to meet more friends, comparing that to the cohort of the Past Masters. It appears that only 5% of the Past Masters joined to meet people. Looking at the survey results for the Brothers who are not active you see that 55% of those Brothers say they joined to meet friends. Looking at the additional feedback from the Brothers who are not active you see that they are extremely interested in both fraternal events and family events... which are things that the Lodge only periodically does. This would infer that if we up the fraternal activities we may be able to hold more men active since over half the inactive Brothers say they were looking for a way to meet friends. In our thought experiment there was a cohort of 20% of the Brothers who are active in the Lodge who are interested in fraternal activities. We may be able to leverage that 20% interest in order to encourage the Brothers who are already active to stand up some fraternal activities that can engage those Brothers who are within a reasonable commute time and were looking for fraternal activities... but are no longer engaged with your Lodge. What else could this tell you? It infers to me that it may be worth asking the active members to do some interesting things to draw the inactive guys who could get to Lodge out and re-engage them. If we discover that the inactive guys are not really interested in degree work perhaps, we look to engage them in activities that involve Masons but fall outside of stated or called communications instead focus on socializing.

What if we were to ask some additional questions? In our hypothetical survey we may see that 75% of the Past Masters and 40% of the Brothers who are active in the Lodge joined because a family member was a Mason. That is a really interesting datapoint. How could we drill down on that a little more? Maybe we want to reach out to the respondents who listed a family member being a Mason as the impetus for their joining and ask them how they found the Lodge. What will they tell us? Perhaps a majority tells us that they did a search for Masonic Lodges close to their homes... that is information that can inform our use of a website and media presence. Maybe a few confide that they have friends and family members who might be interested in the fraternity, which could in turn be the impetus for an event that brings these guys out and has them interacting with the Brethren... because as awesome as a Lodge room is, there are no new Masons in a Lodge room. At the very least it would be worth an outreach to the Brethren to discuss how to talk about Masonry.

Turning back at our hypotheticals we have really looked at only one survey question and by comparing the three cohorts we are able to make inferences into the motivation and behavior of the membership. Make your way through all the questions and ask your own sets of questions. Start with three big ones:

- How does this impact engagement?
- How does this impact membership?
- How can this help us give a better Masonic experience?

As you find yourself making your way through the survey document, look for patterns. This is an opportunity to hear directly from the Brethren on what their motivations are and what they want from their Masonic experience. Listen closely and don't be afraid to ask follow-up questions because if your Brothers want to be involved in Masonry enough to pay dues, they may just be waiting for someone to take an interest in them to take the first step to being more engaged.

A key premise to keep in mind is culture. Each Lodge has its own unique culture which is the glue that binds it together. Over the years the members have come together to construct a Lodge that values a set of things and acts a certain way, and it is not uncommon for two Lodges which are collocated in the same Temple to be radically different in their look and feel. This is by and large the reason why no single program from your Grand Lodge makes an impact at every Lodge throughout the state As there are a handful of challenges that uniquely manifest locally at the Lodges any successful program must speak to the culture of the Lodge if it is going to have any impact. Designing your program with this in mind from the onset dramatically increases your odds of making it work.

Ten

How do I use the Data?

Walking through the survey, consider how you could make the Lodge more interesting and engaging for your Brothers. There are two paths that you can take... doing what you think is going to be interesting or looking at how you can work with the largest number of Brothers and make them feel included and feel part of the Lodge by doing what they would find interesting.

Turning back to our thought experiment we can look at the feedback from the Brethren and draw some conclusions. So many of the men who are members but are not active in the Lodge. In our hypothetical we found that men were interested in fellowship and fraternal activities, might these types of activities serve as a springboard for activities? As a word of caution: you personally may not be a fraternal Mason, your connection to the Lodge might be as a ritualist or an esotericist... and that is ok. Realize that Masons have all manner of interests, and you want to be able to meet the needs of the Brethren (even if they do not necessarily align with your own predilection to delve into the deeper mysteries of the craft). Now in our imaginary responses 20% of the Brothers who are active in the Lodge also said that fraternal activities are important to them. Could you look to them for some assistance in getting something going. Pick up a phone and ask some of your Brothers:

> "Hey Brother, we are trying to get more activities going. We don't have a budget, but we do have a building. Would you be interested in helping me get something going?"

If you receive positive feedback that the Brethren would be interested in helping, put those guys who said they would be interested together! See what ideas come out of the mix. Maybe the Lodge has refreshments before Lodge, but nobody can get there in time to eat. Were you to shift refreshments to after the Lodge meeting might you be able to get more men into a room together? Maybe your Lodge owns its own building, and it is only used four times a month for the Masonic meetings (and twice a month for DeMolay) might you open the Lodge for some other purpose to get the Brothers together? If you can get a few Brothers who are already active to extend that and to do something together in a new way you have an opportunity to invite those Brothers who are not active and fold them into the fun.

Please do not conflate the Lodge meeting with Masonry as a whole. We need to be realistic here, if the Brothers who are not active in the Lodge wanted to go to Lodge meetings, they likely would be going to Lodge meetings. There is something about meetings that does not appeal to every Mason and concentrating on this one aspect of the Masonic experience may not give you the biggest return on your time. Consider this for a moment; you can tweak and make modifications to how meetings are run but what is your potential return going to be? Likely you are going to get pushback from your cohort of Past Masters and alienate some of those members who are already in the room. Those Brothers who get their Masonic experience via Masonic meetings form your baseline engagement and you do not want to risk having them opt out of activities by making changes to the meetings if you do not have to. Big changes get big push back, bit tailored activities speak to the specific whys of Brothers and when people feel heard there is a level of ownership that increases your odds of success.

If you want to make a minor tweak to meetings try any of the following:

- Add some Masonic History to your meeting – You want to keep this as brief as possible. There is a 10 to 15-minute threshold when most Brethren who get their Masonic Experience through the meeting will tune out.
  - Keep it to Masonic Trivia i.e. historical info like famous masons, Masonic places. You can tie it back to a date, something that has arisen in the news (avoiding politics and religion), one of the working tools, something short enough but punchy enough to get

someone's attention. Consider utilizing the Masonic Services Association's short talks.

- Add some Esoterica to your meeting – This is much more difficult because there are many Masons interested in Masonic trivia but very few who are interested in esoteric topics. Consider combining this with a business meeting or getting the business out of the way and then closing lodge and do a presentation after (this gives the audience a chance to leave if this is not the thing for them). You do not want to make your Brothers feel like they are being held hostage.
  - o Philosophy, the biblical links to Masonry… the connection between mystery schools and Masonry. This could be anything a little deeper.
- Try to abbreviate the reading of the minutes. This is a tough one that you want to be wary about. You do not want to alienate your secretary. Secretaries do not grow on trees and if your secretary loves reading the minutes you need to ask yourself if it is worth potentially trying to locate a new secretary to rock the boat.
- Consider the arrival time of your Brothers. Are they able to arrive ahead of the meeting? If you offer refreshments to the Brethren consider having it either before or after the meeting, whichever may give you the most Brothers actually sitting and spending time together.

Whenever you look at making a change you need to ask yourself if the proverbial juice is worth the squeeze or are you getting more participation out of this change than you were prior to its implementation. So try something, run some experiments… and do not be afraid to kill an idea that is not working. You may get some pushback, but let's be real… All of those deep traditions that your Lodge is doing for some reason were all started by a Brother, not unlike yourself, who said I think this idea is going to work and tried it out. But remember you want to align any changes so that they align with the values and culture of the Lodge.

Let us turn back to what we can accomplish with the feedback from the survey.

In our research some of the Brethren may have said that they joined because of a family member. Asking these Brothers for greater detail you discovered that they found the Lodge by performing a simple internet search. My goodness that is valuable data! How can you do something actionable with it? Maybe you can work on a replace yourself program where you teach your Brothers how to speak about their Masonry and then ask the Brethren to talk to friends and family about Masonry… What else could you do? First let us look at how those Brothers found us, they did a web search!

It would be naïve to assume a website will fix all of our problems, but it is our method that's important here. We want to ask why until there are no more why's to ask. This will allow us to get to root causes and our end goal is to automate and systematize as many of the things that we discover. I am going to ask you to think of your own Lodge for a minute. You have had some dynamic Masters and some Masters who have tried hard and seemed to hit a wall. You have had years where there were volunteers coming out of the woodwork and stretches of time where there was nobody to be found to help out. If you can decouple components from the individual Brothers, you can automate sections that are not reliant on a steady stream of regular volunteers. Look for every chance you have to compartmentalize and automate as you make discoveries because this will allow you to concentrate on facilitating and speaking to the Masonic why's of your Brethren instead of burning cycles on infrastructure and support functions. Let's turn back to the discovery on how your Brothers have found the Lodge and continue our thought experiment.

On Websites and Communication

Do you have a website? If you do not, you should strongly consider implementing one that is optimized for your Lodge. Why? Why do you even need a website? What is the goal of your organization in having a web presence? How will it be used and who is it tailored to serve?

A website is a great deal like a house, it is great to get one but then there is the upkeep involved. Once you set it up your site needs to be maintained. There is a school of thought that says post all of your activities to the website at once and the Brothers can go there to see what is going on, job done. That is a terrible idea. Your Lodge has probably been sending trestle boards to its members for decades. Let me ask you this: has receiving a physical copy of all the activities of the Lodge made a discernible difference in your engagement of your Brethren? Most people need to be reminded multiple times of an activity and I pose to you that posting something once and then expecting someone to go looking for what you posted is a sure way to have an event where you and two rather frustrated Wardens are standing alone in a room, effectively having thrown a party that nobody shows up to. Let me share with you a second school of thought: optimize the website as a way for people to find your Lodge and tailor it so that it is a mirror that reflects the things that your members are telling you about why they joined, not just Masonry in general… but your Lodge in particular. They were interested in the Craft but remember it was your Lodge and its culture that they actually bought.

Let us go back to the survey and focus on two motivations: fraternal activities and family who are Masons. You could create a website that tells men where and when your meetings are and highlight two things: fraternal activities and family connections. How could you make the most of these two themes? By creating a page that highlights some of the activities you have done in the past and the types of activities that you are doing in the future. Use pictures so that people visiting your page can see Brothers doing things and by extension identify themselves with Masonry and see themselves at your Lodge. Maybe for the familial theme you uncovered you could have a page or two where a

Brother who has a family connection to Masonry speaks about their family member, the Lodge, and why Masonry is important to them. This would effectively allow you to share the Masonic story of some of the Brethren with as wide an audience as possible. Now with an optimized site, if there are men who are looking for your Lodge or researching their interest in Masonry targeting your geographical area, they can see the types of things that your Lodge culture values, potentially encouraging them to reach out keeping them engaged. This model has you post once and present a vision of your Lodge that men can see themselves in.

Technology is not a be all - end all, and there are many Brothers who will never check their email because they don't have one. For them a physical communication is key, don't forgo a printed communication because your printed media may be the only correspondence a Brother gets from the Lodge other than his dues bill. An engaged member is a dues paying member, please don't forget about those who have embraced Freemasonry but have not embraced technology.

But Charles, if we do this how do we keep the Brethren abreast of what is happening at the Lodge?

My retort is this: if you are lucky one of your hypothetical 100 members is going to go to the website to get the latest and greatest information on what is going on. So you are going to need to decide what is the best use of your time. I would pose to you that the work involved in creating and upkeeping a website for one Brother is not a productive use of your limited resources. I suggest the following: Send an email (using the BCC) of your Lodge activities on the first day of the month to the membership. Send a reminder email the Monday before the meeting/event and then the day of the meeting/event (using the BCC to all of the membership). Look at having one email come from the secretary and one come from you so if a particular Brother starts to disregard the Secretary's emails yours may still catch their eye. This is a way more scalable way to reach out to the members and will end up costing you less time than updating the website regularly. Which you probably don't want to do yourself and which will inevitably Consider using social media to publicize your events to the greater area Facebook makes it as easy as copying and pasting your email content into an event that you can. You only have a finite amount of time to make the most of it. Throw the event out on social media and your Brethren can share the event further through your jurisdiction. There is a caveat; look at your Jurisdiction's rules about the use of social media. There are some Lodges that have developed apps that sit on Brothers' smartphones. This is an interesting development. The challenge you have here is again attention. There are dozens of apps sitting on my iPhone and I really only use a few, the rest get pushed in a folder and unceremoniously forgotten about... the most effective apps have been those which allow for notifications that are pushed to the phone. Look for any opportunity that you can to automate your outreach to get in front of the Brothers eyes. Additional ideas can be gleaned from HubSpot's social media tips. HubSpot is a marketing tool that pivoted into a CRM platform. They have years of resources hidden on their blog, check them out... as I have said before good artists invent, great artists steal.

Eleven

We are a society of friends and Brothers...

You have a homework assignment; you cannot do all these things by yourself, so I am going to ask something of you. One of the things that Masons do not do as much as they once did was travel. The lodges around your own are one of your greatest resources and by getting to know them and visiting their meetings you can find not only friendship but potentially inspiration. Further if you have Brothers who are going through their degrees bringing them along to visit another Lodge is a great opportunity for them to see the degrees again as they move through their catechism, see the world of Masonry is bigger than just your Lodge, and gain a deeper understanding about what they went through when they experienced their own degrees.

Your Lodge likely meets once or twice a month, which means you likely have one or two rehearsals a month so you may have some additional nights free for reconnaissance in force. On one of these off nights consider paying a surrounding Lodge a visit. Arrive before the meeting if possible as many Lodges will have their refreshment before the communication, and you want to be able to talk to the Brethren. Always remember to take a little cash (as some Lodges may put a top hat or a basket out in order to offset the cost of the meal) there may be a meal prior, and they may head out to a local watering hole after. Slide a dues card in your wallet or in your apron case so that you can identify yourself as a Brother and keep your eyes open as you arrive. Observe how the Brothers greet their visitors. What are the topics that they are talking about prior to meeting and how do they socialize as a group? Do you feel welcome? Is there food prior to the meeting? You are watching for anything that could be adopted to improve the experience at your own Lodge. Seek out the Wardens and the Deacons and start up conversations with them. These are good men for you to know because there will come a time when you are going to need some help and many hands make for easy work. Ask them about their Lodge activities and their challenges and share observations about your own Lodge.

Should you be traveling with Brothers who are going through the degrees and have not been raised to the sublime degree of a Master Mason call ahead and ask the Secretary or the Master of the Lodge you are visiting what they are doing the night of your visit as you don't want to arrive with a cohort of EA's and discover the Lodge is conferring the Master Mason degree. If you are not known at the Lodge you are visiting to vouch for your EA or FC Brothers, ask to be examined first and then vouch for those younger Brothers that you are traveling with. Until they get their dues cards, they are going to need your help. If the Lodge you are visiting is operating in a specific degree, talk your traveling companions through any grips and words that they may need to know during the course of the night as you want your younger Brother to be engaged and not embarrassed by forgetting a grip or word during the meeting. Consider asking the Worshipful Master if he needs any help the evening that you are there. Likely they are going to need a hand with a chair... probably a Deacon or a Steward. If the Master does need help and you have a fuller Lodge room, then ask the Master if there is a Brother who can sit with your traveling companions, so they do not feel abandoned. If this is not an option, see if you can sit them closest to the station which you are occupying so they are not alone on the sidelines.

Watch how the Lodge handles its business. Do they hand out the meeting minutes in printed format prior to the meeting? What pieces of business do they have such as coordinating events and doing charity? Do they ask for news on any Brothers or families of departed Brothers? As you hear the meeting minutes note things that interest you, throw a pocket notebook and pen in your jacket pocket. If the Lodge that you are visiting is doing something novel, write it down for later and don't be afraid to ask how it was implemented. After the meeting, ask the Master or the Wardens about a program that interests you. This can lead to a conversation and provide the data needed to evaluate whether this program would be workable at your own

Lodge. How do they interact with their Brethren? Is there anything interesting that happens during the progress of the meeting? How does the closing work? Consider everything that happens, how it would fit into your own Lodge's culture and how it could be adopted and used at a future time by your own Lodge.

As the meeting closes and the Brothers filter out of the Lodge room to hang out, what does their after-Lodge experience feel like? Does everyone head home, or do they head to the refreshment hall or out to a local watering hole? Spend time after Lodge and soak in the after-Lodge experience don't be afraid to ask the Brothers what they are doing and what is working and what has failed along the way. if your conversations uncover something that is working make note of it for your own use. Remember that you need to be cognoscente of your Lodge's culture as some changes are not going to fit the unique culture that your Lodge has built over the years. Strike up conversations with the Wardens and Deacons that you meet and invite them to your Lodge.

Make every effort to visit this Lodge again in the future. Your repeat visits are important for several reasons first and foremost because travel is fun, but you will find that getting to know your Brothers will serve another purpose. Realistically you will at some point you are going to need help at your Lodge and who are you going to ask? Maybe you have a group of young men as your officers, and they all have younger kids and... it's flu season. If you know a group of men, you can reach out for help. You can make calls to fill your chairs instead of walking that panicked lap around the refreshment hall before the meeting and seeing whose arm you can twist to sit in to fill the chairs you this evening. Your visits will create a virtuous cycle... a community of Brothers who know you and are willing to help you. This connection of friendship is a type of implied reciprocity where your interest and assistance to other Lodges pays dividends and helps foster a community that is willing to help each other, but you need to be the change. Imagine that you have put together a degree at your Lodge on an off night because that is the only time that works for your candidate's schedule. If your Lodge has 100 members and you only get 10-15% of the Brothers out, you can invite your surrounding Lodges to the degree. Imagine the impact of seeing not 10 brothers but rather 30-40 Brothers in attendance. You cannot reach out for help unless you know who to call and there is no better way to ask for help than be the guy who shows up to meetings at other local Lodge and always asks where they need help. Traveling gives you exposure to a wider Masonic community and their ideas but your real value is the friendships that you will form along the way.

Twelve

What do I do now that the Brothers want to do things?

There are several questions that you are going to need to think through as you frame your activities. What you want to do, what your Lodge wants to do, and the things you are required to do by your Grand Lodge may be three different things and you need to act accordingly. First look at your jurisdiction's constitution, no... do more than look at it. Read the entire thing. You want to know not only the minimum requirements to function as a Lodge you want to be fluent in what the Constitution says and its application to your Lodge. Understanding what you are required to do and prohibited from doing leaves the third most vital path wide open: everything else. Fluency in the constitution of your jurisdiction ensures that you know what you can or cannot do... which is much better than being told after the fact that you were coloring outside of the lines and being asked to see your dues card.

What degree work am I going to need to do?

You only have so many meetings throughout the course of the year. And you are going to need to get Brothers through the degrees and slip in some other standard meetings like elections or installations. Most Lodges are going to have two meetings a month, and one or two rehearsals. So you are going to be asking your officers to come out at least four nights a month. You want to be cognoscente about the deployment of these officers because you can burn them out. You want to be incredibly careful about what you ask the officers and volunteers to do because they only have so much bandwidth and once you burned out a dedicated Mason out on Masonry the odds are high that you will never see him again. Masonry abhors a vacuum in the Calendar of a Brother. It is a bitter irony that we have kept our dues absurdly low while ever increasing the demand for the most finite of our Brethren's resources: their time. Our system's tendency to relentlessly consume that which fewer Brothers every year seek to selflessly give is one of the greatest threats to the future craft, and one we can control. We burn out our most promising future leaders and are reliant on whatever happens to remain. Can the Craft be surprised with what we reap? But I digress, let's turn our attention back to the calendar.

Your Lodge likely has a Summer recess which will leave you with a total of 16 meetings throughout the year to put on your degrees and programs. That is an exceedingly small cohort of meetings to get a full year of activity done in. Look at the degree work from the prior year. How many candidates came through? Are there any Brothers or candidates that are in process? Consider the experience that you want the Brothers to have. You could perform degree work on multiple candidates, but do you? Could you do more with less by scheduling some degrees on your rehearsal nights and provide a better experience to your Brothers… Could you reach out to some of those Lodge's that you have been visiting and doing joint degrees? You have so many options, your responsibility and your opportunity are in ensuring that a Brother gets the best degree possible. Your call to action is to use all our potential tools to ensure that this happens. If we plot out what degrees you think are going to occur and at what time you think they will happen then you can see what remaining meetings are going to be open for programs. Looking at the calendar dates open for activities based on your remaining meetings is your next task.

What programs do the Brothers want?

The Brothers told you exactly what they were looking for in the survey responses however you cannot do everything at once. This is where the culture component comes in. Consider that the component parts of your Lodge all have their own motivations in what they value and if you want to maintain and increase engagement you will need to align the activities that you are planning with what the Lodge will want and what they will respond to. Having spoken to the Past Masters you have heard a little about what was working the years they found themselves in the Oriental chair. Hopefully you also heard what was not working the year that they were the Master of the Lodge because those who don't learn from history are doomed to repeat it. What events and programs are long-standing that you could tweak to make them more appealing? Speak to some of the old timers and perhaps you will uncover a Lazarus program[4], one of those programs that just faded away (you know they type of program that everyone recalls fondly but one that just does not happen any longer for some reason) that could yield rewards if revived.

There really is nothing new under the sun my Brother and you will find that the memories of the Lodge may be your truest guide. Think of the conversations that you had with the Brothers from the Lodges that you have visited. What can you leverage for the Brethren? The programs that other Lodges are putting on are wonderful resources as you can likely obtain a template and just copy it for execution at your own Lodge. Is there a Grand Master's award in your jurisdiction awarded to exemplary Lodges? What steps do you need to put together to achieve this distinction? These programs are great resources that you can leverage to engage your Brothers. There is however a caveat that you need to consider. Depending on the situation at your Lodge and the total number of Brothers willing to lend a hand you need to balance the capabilities and potential stress to your Lodge with short term achievement. Meaning this, you do not want to burn out the handful of Brothers that are willing to help your Lodge simply to achieve a goal in one year which will then take several years to recover from. It is ok to proportionally achieve goals… the audacious long-term goal is a stronger Lodge that is resilient enough to stand the test of time with that in mind considering what steps you can take to achieve in the near term while not jeopardizing that audacious goal for the Lodge's future.

How are you going to define your success?

Success is defined by you and your Lodge. Our goal is ultimately sustainable success and if you are looking for a measure, consider a measurement like having the attendees to Lodge events equal or exceed the average attendance. You can hit some home runs that fill your Lodge room with Brothers however

---

[4] Lazarus program - A program that you can revive from the dead for the benefit of your Lodge.

it is easier to win a game with singles and doubles. Incremental wins are sustainable. I would pose to you that a great deal of burnout in Masonic Leadership is caused by Brothers being inspired to greatness but having their success measured against the metrics of the 1950's when it seemed as if nearly every man was a Freemason and when the fourth of July parades in every town found Masonic components stretching one mile long and ten men abreast. Define your success by moving the Lodge forward or engaging some larger portion of the Brethren than you had the prior year. If you can hand a sustainable path forward to the Brothers who come after you the Lodge will be set up to be more successful than most. There is a Japanese concept of Kaizen that is worth looking at as a philosophy for steady incremental progress that is worth looking at as an improvement philosophy. Consider how you can incrementally improve; you don't need to do it all at once. Let's see what we can learn from best practices in Japan.

What is Kaizen? - Five S of Kaizen

"Kaizen" refers to a Japanese word which means "improvement" or "change for the better". Kaizen is defined as a continuous effort by each and every employee (from the CEO to field staff) to ensure improvement of all processes and systems of a particular organization. Work for a Japanese company and you would soon realize how much importance they give to the process of Kaizen. The process of Kaizen helps Japanese companies to outshine all other competitors by adhering to certain set policies and rules to eliminate defects and ensure long term superior quality and eventually customer satisfaction.

Kaizen works on the following basic principle.

"Change is for good".

Kaizen means "continuous improvement of processes and functions of an organization through change". In a layman's language, Kaizen brings continuous small improvements in the overall processes and eventually aims towards organization's success. Japanese feel that many small continuous changes in the systems and policies bring more effective results than few major changes. The Kaizen process aims at continuous improvement of processes not only in the manufacturing sector but all other departments as well. Implementing Kaizen tools is not the responsibility of a single individual but involves every member who is directly associated with the organization. Every individual, irrespective of his/her designation or level in the hierarchy needs to contribute by incorporating small improvements and changes in the system.

"Five S" of Kaizen is a systematic approach which leads to foolproof systems, standard policies, rules, and regulations to give rise to a healthy work culture at the organization. You would hardly find an individual representing a Japanese company unhappy or dissatisfied. Japanese employees never speak ill about their organization. Yes, the process of Kaizen plays an important role in employee satisfaction and customer satisfaction through small continuous changes and eliminating defects. Kaizen tools give rise to a well-organized workplace which results in better productivity and yields better results. It also leads to employees who strongly feel attached towards the organization.

Let us understand the five S in Detail:

SEIRI - SEIRI stands for Sort Out. According to Seiri, employees should sort out and organize things well. Label the items as "Necessary",`` Critical", `` Most Important", "Not needed now ``,"Useless `` and so on. Throw what all is useless. Keep aside what all is not needed at the moment. Items which are critical and most important should be kept at a safe place.

SEITION - Seition means to Organize. Research says that employees waste half of their precious time searching for items and important documents. Every item should have its own space and must be kept at its place only.

SEISO - The word "SEISO" means to shine in the workplace. The workplace ought to be kept clean. Declutter your workstation. Necessary documents should be kept in proper folders and files. Use cabinets and drawers to store your items.

SEIKETSU-SEIKETSU refers to Standardization. Every organization needs to have certain standard rules and set policies to ensure superior quality.

SHITSUKE or Self Discipline - Employees need to respect organization's policies and adhere to rules and regulations. Self-discipline is essential. Do not attend office in casuals. Follow work procedures and do not forget to carry your identity cards to work. It gives you a sense of pride and respect for the organization.

Kaizen focuses on continuous small improvements and thus gives immediate results.[5]

What Ideas does Kaizen give you for your Lodge? If you have 16 meetings a year what would your Lodges Freemasonry feel like if there was one improvement made in the experience of the Brethren at every meeting? Imagine how small changes for the better made every meeting every year for years would impact your Lodge, now imagine what the Craft would look like were every Lodge in a jurisdiction adopt the practice.

Who will come?

Q: Who will come to these activities?

A: Who did you ask?

I am going to level with you. If you want to expand the attendees past the group of Brothers who get their version of Masonic experience from attending meetings, you are going to have to invite people. Pick up the phone and actually call your Brothers. You can email them or send them a text but the odds for engagement in these methods are exceptionally low. Look at the survey results and consider who is interested in the specific type of activity

---

[5] Juneja, P. (n.d.). MSG Management Guide. Retrieved April 5, 2020, from https://www.managementstudyguide.com/what-is-kaizen.htm

that you are working on as these are the Brethren that you can reach out to. This is not a one and done process, you are going to have to repeatedly remind people and ask them to attend. You are going to need to inform people several times more often than you would think that a reasonable person would need to be informed. You want to announce at least 3-4 months out and be cognoscente to invite the Brothers who would be interested in this type of activity. Send out a manifest of activities happening that month and give the Brethren a rolling forecast of the activities coming over the next 3-4 months. This will give the Brothers insight into what is happening at their Lodge and increase the odds of attendance by scheduling time to attend.

Consider opening your activities to other Lodges. The ability to combine the activities of several Lodges not only makes the event bigger but it creates a novelty that in turn creates excitement. This is a virtuous cycle where more Brothers attending encourages more to come out which in turn increases the probability that you will meet the metrics for event success that you set out earlier. Teaming with other Lodges can be extended throughout the functions of a Lodge because it is easier to fill a room or an event by pulling potential attendees from several Lodges.

How much will it cost?

Your jurisdiction probably has a formal budgeting process where you need to generate an annual budget and share it with the Lodge for approval. Let us consider how we conceptualize the costs of our activities. What if we only had two variables in the form of costs we are going to incur and costs we 'might' incur. If there are monthly, quarterly, or annual costs that always happen, build them into the budget. Maybe your Lodge has light refreshments at every meeting. What are your monthly costs for those meals? Are there opportunities to use the total cost of the meals over the course of the year to buy the Lodge a better experience? Perhaps there is a local business that could cater your meetings to raise quality and lower the logistics that the Lodge needs to coordinate? Is there a Brother who runs a catering company who you could leverage? Can you recoup some of the cost by putting out a donation hat at every meal? Consider how you can either pool cost or how you could recoup cost in creative ways. You could apply the same logic to say candidates' aprons and bibles, if you only have a few candidates a year consider not buying your candidate supplies one off and pooling the cost for a single purchase to lower the cost basis for the Lodge.

This logic can be applied to the cost basis for variable or one-off events. Look at opportunities to purchase simplicity. Can you outsource portions of the event logistics like food, drinks, or labor?

The hidden cost of events is going to be engagement. Not the engagement of getting your members to take part per se but engagement of volunteers until burnout. With a smaller cohort of members who are active in Masonic activities there is a natural tendency to use the same eager Brothers over and over. Everything you ask a Brother to help with comes at the cost of something he may not be able to assist with in the future, there is finite time, and every ask has an opportunity cost. Don't ask the same guys for everything; this would be a tacit mistake. Your volunteers are a resource that has to be carefully managed. If you have a newly raised Master Mason, be wary of handing him a Deacon's staff and a ritual book but consider his 'why' for joining in the first place and see if you can align that 'why' with an open need that your Lodge has. Careful and considerate is the path that will leave the least Brothers feeling overwhelmed with Masonry.

Remember the 24-inch gauge. We all have a finite amount of time, and we must manage it the best that we can. By aligning your team with their why's and treating them like a resource that you don't want to squander you are less likely to see burn-out and be able to have those Brothers continuing to assist the Lodge years into the future.

One of the hardest resources for you to manage is going to be the enthusiasm of your newly raised Brothers. They are going to want to do everything and complete every petition. In a world with declining membership this is a road to burnout. There is a vast legion of Masonic bodies that would love to have their energy to solve the challenges presented by fewer members across the Craft as a whole help them find outlets that best meet **their** needs. The Blue Lodge is here to make Masons and you can best do that by aligning the why of these new Brothers with activities that can help them achieve their goals. Activities are an easy outlet for these men to contribute to the craft, but their participation will vary depending on the particular Brother's interests. Consider a central way for you to help your new Brothers is to help them not overcommit themselves to the detriment of themselves, your Lodge, and the Craft itself.

Thirteen

How do we pay for all of this?

Prudent planning and being able to determine the costs of the experience that you are working to establish is going to be a key factor in your success. You need to look at the big picture and understand both what costs you cannot avoid and what cash flows you can anticipate so let's walk through this. Your jurisdiction likely has a budgeting function built into the way that it directs how Lodge expenses are reported to your membership and perhaps the Grand Lodge, so these are factors that you are going to need to build into your planning.

You want to determine how much you have to spend and understand the costs you can't do anything about… laying those costs that are outside of your control to the side. These costs would be things like Grand Lodge assessments or if you don't have a holding company building related items like utility bills. Some costs are effectively outside your control so you want to concentrate your time on the costs that can create a better experience for your Brothers. I would advocate looking at zero based accounting when you put your budget together. Begin by pretending that you are starting your Lodge today. What would your budget look like if you didn't just copy and paste the expenditures from last year in this year's plan? What expenses are necessary to support the engagement of your members? Start by looking at those activities that have the hearts and minds of your members (those items that could negatively impact the participation or emotional investment of the Brethren were you not to do them). This would be an opportunity to reach out and speak to that decade worth of Past Masters again to understand the prior years' expenditures and who worked on the programs that they support. Doing things because we have always done these things is a path to stagnation. The budget process gives you an opportunity to see if the proverbial juice is worth the squeeze for all Lodge activities. The odds are high that if not one of those Past Masters in the past decade remember why you are doing something that appears in the budget you may be safe in removing said item from your budget.

Let's look at mechanics:

You have x number of Brothers paying $y number of dues annually, multiplying this out you will get the total amount of income that you can work with. You may have diversified income streams from investments or rental income… outstanding put them to the side for a moment. A portion of your dues income goes to some recurring costs that are unique to your Lodge and jurisdiction, what is the remainder? That remainder is the amount of cash that you have in order to fund the activities of your Lodge. Consider those activities that you are going to fund at a loss and those you want to break even on. There are going to be some things, dinners for instance, that members may expect because you have always provided them with the cash to improve them. Would it make sense to have dinners on degree or program nights and to shift to light refreshments on business meeting nights? You have the power of the pen. On those items that you want to break even on you are going to want to recoup your cost. For those types of events get your cash up front, cash up front ensures that the Brother outlying his reservation will show up (as he has outlaid cash) and will ensure that your Lodge has not spent money that is going to be a net loss. When a Brother pays upfront the Lodge doesn't end up holding the bag.

Looking to the future and to saving to support the Lodge let's look back at those costs that you are going to have to deal with, those externalities you cannot control. Are there ways to reduce the cost? Could you spend some money on the front end to reduce the recurring cost? Perhaps you could switch to LED lighting to reduce your utility bills or look to investments in electronic thermostats to lower your utility bills. If you own your building are there out of the box things that you can do to offset your costs such as solar panels or leasing your roof rights to cellular companies. Can you go to online trestle boards to reduce the mailing costs that you are bearing? There are options to reduce your costs and each of those saved dollars to provide your Lodge additional funding for its activities.

Again, you may have prior years of budgets to refer to. I do not recommend copying them directly. I am going to ask you to consider using something called zero based budgeting that I had mentioned earlier. Pretend that this is the first year that you have ever had a Lodge and you were starting from scratch. What things are profoundly important for the Lodge to spend money on? Starting from a blank slate is a way to ensure that you are not carrying forward decisions that were made years ago (because we have always done it) that may not actually be providing any tangible return or support your Lodge's culture.

Let's think outside of the box for a moment. Your Lodge has been around for some time. Do you believe that it will be in existence for years to come? We get caught in a trap when planning for our Lodges on being laser focused on the short term. Why? I would pose that as Master only serves for a limited time it's a natural mode of thought but the lifespan of a Lodge can be centuries so what would the impact be if we thought in those terms? Your Lodge may or may not have investments or funds set aside for a rainy day and you may run so lean on dues that you do not think you could afford it. Past performance is no guarantee of future results but let's say your Lodge invested $50 a year for a century in an index fund based just on the Dow Jones Industrial Average... which happened to grow at ~5% over the past 124 years. If we do some back of the napkin math, investing $50 a year over 100 years at 5% annual growth would have your Lodge investing $5,000 in principle over the century and yielding ~$132k in gains... transforming your slow and steady $50 a year set aside for the future into an account work ~$137k. Run a thought experiment and consider a century from now your Lodge meeting to discuss the fact that there is a new furnace needed. How would they pay for it? You could hope that over the next 100 years Brothers leave bequests to the Lodge, but the odds are that those windfalls are going to be spent quickly after they are received on operational items. Consider how you can impact the Lodges future for the

Brethren who have not even been born yet and consider building in an annual investment percentage of total dues received and baking into your bylaws that unless otherwise directed by the donor a set percentage of all bequests and donations are automatically deposited in a long-term investment account for your Lodge.

Turning back to those Lodges that are lucky enough to have multiple income streams, what percentage of those income streams can you forgo in the near term? If you can reduce consumption even $50 you can help save for a rainy day. Consider reexamining your bylaws and creating permanent committees or boards of trustees to manage your money and invest long-term.

There is one last bit of budget advice that I have for you. I call it the voice of the budget. Ask a Brother who always comes to Lodge to be your voice of fiscal diligence. You will receive inquiries for donations throughout the course of the year which may or may not be expected and likely are not budgeted. When the Secretary reads an appeal for a $100 advertisement in some other organization's program there will be someone stand up and inevitably make a motion to donate, the voice of the budget would ask the WM if the cost is in the budget. This pause gives the Lodge a chance to actually see if there are unallocated funds that can support the donation. Everyone wants to be charitable, and it is easy to be charitable with other people's money... The money you are stewarding at your Lodge is for the men who have not even knocked on the West Gate yet. Be relentless in supporting the unique flavor of Masonry which is your Lodge but to try to sock away a little something for the men who come after you.

Fourteen

I can't do this alone, how do I ask for help?

Asking for help is hard for some and impossible for others, but it is a skill you are going to need to develop. You cannot do it all alone... you can try for a while, but this is likely going to lead you to burn-out yourself and that isn't going to help Masonry. Your Brethren are not mind readers and the truth is that many of our Brethren's idea of getting involved stopped at filling out their petition to join the Masons in the first place, subsequently there may not be Brothers coming out of the woodwork to help you coordinate Lodge activities. It doesn't matter how amazing your ideas are if they don't ever get out of your head your successful execution is going to be predicated on the ability to engage your Brothers. That is where getting to know the Brethren comes in. If you can get a glimpse into what motivates a Brother to join the fraternity and what they are interested in you are going to be more successful in asking them to assist you in x, y, or z.

Looking at the total population of things needing to be done, what items can you reasonably do yourself? While you cannot do all of it, that does not preclude you from doing some of it. But out of the multitude of things that need to be done, how do you decide what it is something that you can do? Look at the population of actions and consider those things that if someone else does them it will directly lead that Brother to be more engaged and feel a heightened sense of ownership of the Lodge. Could this task help the Brother fulfill their Masonic why? If the Brother that you were going to ask to help with something would get more out of some other activity, consider doing the initial item yourself. These fallback items are tasks that you are comfortable or capable of doing yourself... that you are willing to take one for the team and perform yourself so you can deploy the limited number of Brothers you can count on to do things that really matter. The year I served in the East my fallback items were folding communications, stuffing envelopes for mailing, and taking out the trash. Often when I was Master Brothers would comment that I should not be gathering garbage and taking it to the dumpster and my reply would be "I would rather have the Brethren do more meaningful things." Since the Brothers only have so much bandwidth part of your job is to guard their capacity and deploy it like the precious resource that it is. Matching the right Brother with the right task will keep him going and ready to be asked again where matching a Brother with the wrong task will turn an opportunity to help into a burden and decrease the probability that they will help in the future.

Draft out how many people you are going to need to perform the work necessary for a given event. When you consider the time required for an activity do not just consider the time needed to do the work (including set-up and teardown) just as important is the consideration as to whether the Brothers who are helping will actually be able to enjoy the event that you are planning. Asking for twice the volunteers would allow you to halve their committed time and open up more time for them to enjoy what you are planning. If possible, look for ways to outsource the work, take an event for Lodge significant others as an example. Would it make more sense to ask people to help put on your own event or more sense to use a local restaurant so you can leverage their staff and facilities? Perhaps the challenge is that even after reflecting on the 'whys' of the Brethren you still cannot come up with a list of enough bodies to assist. In these cases ask yourself this, "If we are working on an event for the Brethren does it matter which Brethren?" Having traveled to your neighboring Lodges your phone is now your friend. Can you partner with the local Lodge and have a dual or tri-Lodge event? Fixating on who gets credit will severely limit your ability to get things done... Other than the officers of both Lodges nobody is likely going to remember that the event was not hosted solely by your Lodge. The Brothers attending your amazing event are going to remember that there was a fun Masonic activity that was well attended. Solomon imported his workers from Tyre to achieve his goals, there is nothing wrong with following his precedent to achieve yours.

So how do you ask for some help? You are going to need to pick up a phone and ask for it. Sorry. Sending an e-mail or a text is not going to cut it because these can be ignored or deferred until it is conveniently too late to participate. When you use one of these more convenient communications methods you are going to get a Brother to consider your ask as an option. It's a volunteer organization so if what you are working on is worth the time to actually go through with it is worth giving the Brother a call. Your ask can be as simple as calling and saying:

> "Brother Charles,
>
> The Lodge is working on 'X', and we could use some help. You have mentioned that you were interested in having the Lodge do 'Y'. This seems like something that you may be really good at doing, would you be able to help me?

It can be that easy, but you are going to need to give it some thought and look for things you need help with that parallel the interests or strengths of your Brothers. Do not leave a voicemail asking for help. A voicemail is an option to assist when you call someone or are speaking to them live, they have to tell you no, call them back. Any ask that you make is going to include several components: that the Lodge needs them, that you think they may be interested in this thing, that you think they may be good at this thing… and a call to action (actually asking for their help). When you ask for help you are sharing that they Lodge needs them, that the Brother you had been speaking to has expressed an interest in and you heard their interest. You are affirming that it is something that they could be good at, and you are tying it all back to the fact that you personally need this help. This approach demonstrates the value of the Brother you are asking and shows how it is helping both you and your Lodge. Ask and you shall receive… Upon careful examination I realize that there is no specific percentage of success spelled out in this biblical passage, but your success rate will approach zero if you don't step out of your comfort zone to ask.

Fifteen

We have done all this work. How do I keep it going?

You have put together all this work so how do you ensure that it continues next year?

You don't create an environment where institutional inertia does.

Here are a few rules of thumb that will help the Brothers keep this moving forward:

- Be cognoscente of people's time throughout the year.
- Thank the Brothers helping at each event.
- Send out a Summary email of how an event was coordinated and who did what job to all your volunteers ensuring the Lodge can collectively run with the ball in the future.
- At the end of the year send a thank you note to your volunteers for the work they have done.
- Work on a ten-year plan for your Lodge.

A ten-year plan sounds like a crazy amount of work, but it is not if you break it into its component parts.

Let us walk through one I did for my own Lodge. My comments will be listed in bold italics; you will find an unmarked version at the end of this text.

Ten Year Plan

Palestine Lodge 2018-2028

What is the purpose of your plan and what are you hoping to accomplish?

Knowing where we are going is contingent on understanding where we are, and the challenges that are on our immediate horizon. This document shall consist of a summary of the situation and strategy, our community, externalities, near/long term recommendations, and a conclusion.

Our Environment

Let's describe the community in which our Lodge is located and the area within a 15-minute drive to our building. Look to demographic information on the area, this data can often be found on websites geared towards the real estate industry or even the US census data.

Catonsville is a vibrant small town, with younger couples moving in and starting families yet over the past several years we have seen new membership inquiries slow, so where are all of the petitions?

The 21228-zip code is a desirable area with good schools. The average age of the residents is ~39.1 years old and males make up, so Catonsville at first glance appears to be a good fit for fraternalism, however demographics (our own and our communities) require planning and strategic action on our part to preserve Catonsville Masonry through the 21st Century.

Our Challenge

What are the demographic issues that your Lodge is facing? Consider your membership and who your target is for membership. How will your Lodge compete for the time and interest of men who may be interested in the fraternity?

In 1955 a fortune 500 company could expect to be in business for 75 years, in 2017 the fortune 500 can expect to be in business for 15 years.

The world has changed, and this change is permanent.

The expectations of Gen X and Millennials are based on a subscription economy. They do not pay for movies or music, they stream it. They expect ongoing value for their time. They expect memorable experiences, and they expect relationships. If your product or organization does not deliver on these expectations, they will not tell you they are disappointed, they will vote with their feet.

That level of change, and service seems impossible to deliver. But Palestine needs to focus not on what it cannot do but what it can do but what it can provide that nobody else can.

Applied Masonry

What is your mission? How will your Lodge look to embody Freemasonry?

In our ritual we describe two types of Masonry

- Operative masonry - the building of structures
- Speculative masonry - Using the tools and emblems of the builder's trade to build moral character

There are no new Masons in Lodge rooms, if we conflate good Masonry with good Lodge attendance, we are putting the mechanics of the fraternity ahead of its ends.

We have to practice applied Masonry. This applied Masonry is practicing Brotherly Love, Relief, and Truth in the world. This is how we will form relationships with men looking for what we have to offer. What we do in the Lodge room is a dress rehearsal, we need to be seen being Masons, and practicing the fraternal bond.

Our Strategy

How will we attract men who may be looking for what Masonry has to offer?

To successfully attract and retain men in the 21st Century we need to focus on them and how Masonry can align with their goals. This will require the Lodge to practice putting the man first. To succeed and grow we must approach the world, and every man who we meet with two questions:

1. Whence Came You? - Who is the candidate and where are they coming from?
2. What Came You Here to Do? - What are their expectations and what are they looking for?

Palestine needs to begin the relationship with a potential new member by focusing on how we can help them find those things, and if we cannot help them have the integrity to refer them to someone who can.

Through our ritual we can provide an experience like no other, we must continue to provide an excellent experience.

Through our Brothers we can provide real friendships in a world of single serving friends.

We must not conflate attending Lodge with being a good Mason; it is integral for us to practice actual applied Masonry, because there are no new Masons in Lodge rooms.

Consider this: After the battle of Opequon, McKinley accompanied a surgeon to visit a Confederate soldier taken prisoner at the battle. McKinley stated:

Almost as soon as we passed the guard, I noticed that the doctor shook hands with a number of Confederate prisoners. He also took from his pocket a roll of bills and distributed all he had among them. Boy-like, I looked on in wonderment; I did not know what it meant. On the way back to our camp I asked him, "Did you know these men or ever see them before?" "No," replied the doctor, "I never saw them before." "But how did you know them and why did you give them money?", I asked. "They are Masons, and we Masons have ways of finding that out." "But" I persisted, "you gave them a lot of money, all you had about you. Do you ever expect to get it back?" "Well," said the doctor, "if they are ever able to pay it back, they will. But it makes no difference to me. They are brother Masons in trouble, and I am only doing my duty." I said to myself, "If that is Masonry, I will take some of it myself."

If men are looking for friends, if they are looking for something bigger than themselves our strategy is to show those facets of the fraternity to them.

Our strategy is succinctly Masonry practiced in plain view.
Our strategy is to put the Brother at the center of what we do.

A Lodge is a number of Brethren, the building is where we confer degrees, and the world is where we practice Masonry.

Palestine Today:

What is the situation today with your Lodge? What does your membership look like and where are those Brothers?

Our current membership number is: 190
We have had one Brother called from labor and one Brother passed to the Degree of Fellowcraft
Out of the 58 Brothers receiving their Master Mason Degree, seven are Catonsville residents the remaining 88% of the Brothers are from the surrounding zip codes. Out of our total membership only ~16.2% resides within Catonsville the remaining 83% reside outside of 21228, 74.8% of our membership live within the state of Maryland.

What are the demographics of your Lodge membership? What are their ages, by knowing their ages we can determine how long these Brothers will be with us?

Looking at our membership mix are members are predominantly retirees, which is typical:

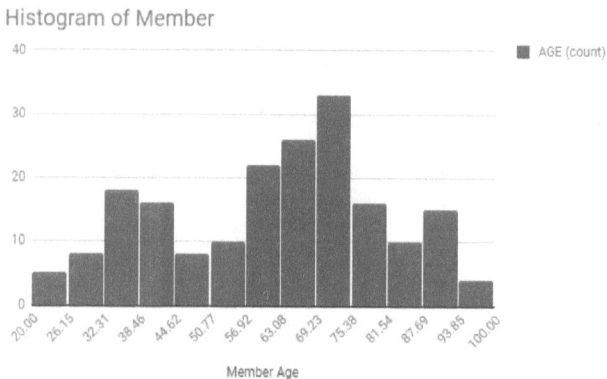

Demographics drive our future. The average life expectancy in the US is ~78.4 years old. Based on our member mix we should expect ~43.9% of our Brothers to be called from labor in the period between 2018 and 2028.

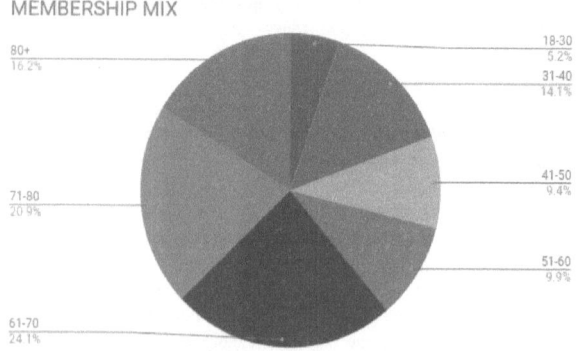

The reality is that Palestine is healthier than many Lodges in the jurisdiction and if we act now the Lodge can actively plan now to preserve Catonsville Masonry.

Membership Goals:

What are we working to do with this plan?

- Understand the community in which the Lodge resides
- Identify long term trends that may impact Lodge growth
- Identify a strategy to slowly grow membership to ensure lodge viability
  - Present engagement tactics for increasing membership
  - Identify short-term tactics to retain membership

Catonsville, MD

What are the demographics of our community, who is moving in and why? If we can determine their ages, we can determine their motivations. In the case of Catonsville the homes and schools are the draw, this creates a challenge in that young Dads are focused on being Dad's and this may not be conducive to Lodge engagement. We need to understand our community in order to understand what we are working with.

Catonsville has had a real estate boom, with younger couples purchasing housing stock to gain access to a safe small town with good schools at a far lower cost of entry than neighboring Howard County.

The population of our community is ~36.7k, some 47% of the population is male. With an average age of ~39 in Catonsville, first glance would have Catonsville filled with men of perfect age for Masonry.

The average age of a first-time father is now 30 years old; the parenting load does not start to decrease until the high school years. Making fathers likely to be unable to join due to parental commitments until they reach the age of 45-49 and their children do not require the same level of engagement.

Looking at the real estate trends Catonsville is desirable for young families, however the limited housing stock and later age in starting a family is creating a population of men who are likely unable to actively consider Masonry until their mid-late forties.

Catonsville has a high density of churches, and while belief in a supreme being is a requirement for joining the craft, several mainstream religious organizations actively encourage men not to join the fraternity. The most widely known is the Papal Bull discouraging Catholics from joining Freemasonry, with ~19.4% of Catonsville residents identifying as Catholic and adding Southern Baptists, 7th Day Adventists, Pentecostals, and Muslims we look at ¼ of Catonsville residents belonging to faiths which either actively discourage or may not view favorably the craft.

Taking all of the variables into account the population of eligible men in Catonsville, who are unlikely to die over the next decade is: 8,760, of which 6,084 are of the ages most likely to be actively engaged in raising a family. This leaves a much-reduced target population of 2,676 men who are of the right age and unlikely to be affiliated with a religious denomination unsupportive of Freemasonry. Further, a sampling of tax records of single-family homes with 2-3 bedrooms shows them as selling at regular 4–5-year intervals, while additional research is required. Initial research suggests that young families are regularly moving making the potential target population smaller than the ~2.6k anticipated by examining the demographics.

The demographics of Catonsville have roughly ⅓ of eligible men likely to die within the next 10-15 years, ⅓ actively raising families (whom Masonry likely will not be an option). To continue viability the Lodge must seek out ways to get in front of and engage the target population of 2k men.

Target Demographic

Who are we looking at as potential new Brothers, what do we know about them? Some basic research into age cohorts and the motivation of different age groups will assist you in understanding the call of the different generations which could potentially benefit from Masonry.

The average age for a man to get married now is 28 years old, the average age to start a family is 31. Any membership program must deliver on the experience expected. Given that most members polled made some reference to making friends the Lodge's ability to deliver on this experience will be best done by focusing on men in their late forties who have less of a parenting burden, and those men who are reaching 65-68 who find themselves with no community as they move from the world of professional work life to retirement. Men in their twenties will move an average of 11 times in their lifetimes and may not be retained. While men in the ages between 28-31 will likely start families, it would be advisable to target those men who are not married or childless via Facebook advertising to attract these potential long-term members.

Commute Time

Commute time is key. You have calculated the mean commute time earlier in your research. You want to capture this detail so you can keep this in the minds of your Brethren and plan around the real burden that transit costs working men.

Reviewing the sign in book at Palestine for the past decade reveals two trends, attendance rarely exceeds 10% of our membership. Outside of the Past Masters of the Lodge, the Brothers who attend live an average of ~15 minutes' drive from the Lodge.

In our Metro area the average commute is anywhere from 30-45 minutes each way. Non-retired Members have already spent between 1 and 1.5 hours in a car prior to their commute to Lodge. This would create a circumference of membership, with the Lodge in the center. And extending to Ellicott City, Catonsville, Halethorpe, Arbutus, and Columbia.

Internet Trends

What is the environment that you are operating in? What is happening digitally? Earlier we hypothesized that many members who are active found the Lodge via the web... what else could they have found. What is your plan for standing out and being noticeable? This is where you want to map out your plan for how you will appear when searched for online.

Over the past several years the Grand Lodge of Maryland has been actively advertising across the state, this and the Grand Lodge investment in Websites and social media has created an environment where men who would have located Palestine are more easily locating the MWGL of MD. This is good for the craft; however the Grand Lodge parses their inquiries and sends them out to the constituent Lodges based on the geographical location of the inquirer. Palestine has over the past decade gained brothers from outside of Catonsville, with 50% of them being introduced to Palestine by a friend or family member and the remainder locating the Lodge by finding us online. There is a direct correlation in the decrease in Palestine's web petitioners and the improvement of the Grand Lodge's web efforts and the implementation of their referral program. Unless the Grand Lodge changes their web strategy the internet shall not be a major membership driver for the foreseeable future.

It would be advisable to review the web presence and consider its intention. Members are probably not going to go to the Lodge to learn about the Lodge. The more effective marketing approach would be to have any web presence be focused on the potential new member and provide picture rich stories about how men in our target demographics have realized the values we have identified as our cultural touchstones.

For example, a photo selection of a Brother in his thirties and a man in his sixties on a page discussing the traditions of the Lodge. A photo selection of a Dad in his forties on a page discussing being part of something larger than themselves. A photo selection of Brothers of all ages discussing the fraternal aspects of the craft.

A series of landing pages should be created interviewing a handful of Brothers of all backgrounds discussing why they came to the fraternity, what they expected, and why they stay.

A contact us link that has some mystery such as: Could Masonry be for you? Or Interested, every journey begins with a first step. This should be the link that most draws the eye.

"A wealth of information creates a poverty of attention ..." —Herbert A. Simon

Who we are and how we can help a potential Brother meet his goals is the only message that matters? Any content that does not support membership is superfluous. Lists of Officers and Past Masters do not provide value to the man who is looking for something in Masonry and are focused on the Lodge and not the potential candidate.

When a man comes to our site looking for friendship and to be part of a tradition bigger than himself this should be exactly what they find. Palestine's history and traditions should all be presented in such a way as to support the intentions of the potential member coming to the site.

Due to the number of men moving in and out of our immediate area a special visitors section would be advisable that would invite traveling Masons to our Lodge, discuss the meeting times, and tell the visiting Brother what they should bring with them. The call to action should be: Welcome Brother - Contact us to coordinate a visit.

Membership Strategy

What is your plan for being open to new Brothers, how will you find men who can benefit from what the Lodge has to offer? Here we want to talk about what our Lodge can do to make men more aware of the craft. How will new Masons be found, and our existing Brethren retained?

The Lodge needs to hold onto its current members and grow large enough to remain viable. Viability is not the same a size, to avoid membership crashes in the future the Lodge has to grow no larger than the community can support, conceivably big enough to fund programs but small enough that one Brother could conceivably know every other member. Were the Lodge to grow over 300 members, it is likely time to form another Lodge to avoid future membership crunches that threaten the Lodge's existence.

To be successful the Lodge will push itself out into the community to make men **aware** of Masonry. The burden for this will largely fall on younger men, because the Lodge needs to project itself as a mirror that potential members can see themselves in. If men want to make friends through the fraternal aspects of Masonry and be part of something bigger than themselves that is what we need to project.

The Lodge will specifically **target and engage** men in different life stages to bring them to the fraternity.

The Lodge will **retain** its members by continuing to provide programs they show interest in and reaching out to Brothers from out of state.

Not everyone who knocks gets in, not every man is going to get something out of Masonry and far fewer are going to be worth investing our finite resources in.

NEAR TERM TACTICS

Here we want to plot out what things the Lodge can do in the near term to meet its strategic goals? What steps can you take incrementally to meet your goals?

Using Grand Lodge inquiries and interests from the community the Lodge's goal would be to bring in an equal number of men as Masons as we lose to Non-payment of dues or death. The Brothers under 50 must actively look to produce a number of petitions equal to the number of men whom we would anticipate being called from labor over the next decade.

1. Identify our Lodge Culture. I would recommend focusing on fellowship and ritual. A large percentage of the brethren identified making friends as their motivation to join as well as being part of something bigger than themselves. These are aspects that the Lodge can deliver on if Palestine plans activities with them in mind.
2. Identify what we want the Lodge to look like in the future. Because most of our target audience only has a vague idea that Masonry even exists the Lodge can paint its own narrative. The Lodge identifying fellowship and ritual as key attributes should create a web presence that is not focused on the Lodge, rather focused on the men coming to the Lodge.
3. Focus on Columbia and Ellicott City as potential sources of membership. The population of each area is larger than Catonsville however the mix of housing in terms of single-family homes, multi-tenant housing, and townhomes as well as the number of unmarried or divorced men of all ages makes these communities potential hot spots for Masonry.
   1. Engagement should be in the form of being seen in the community. For the unmarried man, these areas are suitcase communities so the Lodge's time would be better spent having masons meet in areas where men frequent

2. Facebook advertising to these areas would also be recommended. This advertising would take the form of keywords.

    1. A poll amongst the under 50 Brothers as well as the 65-68 cohort would be needed. The survey would ask them to describe themselves and their interests in single words. I.e. sports, history, philosophy. Facebook will allow us to micro target the desired audience for a very moderate cost ($20 a quarter)

0. It has been increasingly difficult to connect with interested men and have them visit the Lodge. If we coordinate monthly meet ups that rotate through Ellicott City, Columbia, and Old Ellicott City the Lodge can invite men expressing interest to meet us on their own territory and form a relationship with us early on. Asking the gentleman to come to the building is convenient for us and does not put his experience first.

a. These meetups, not taking place on Lodge nights, could engage the Brothers who might not be interested in the Lodge experience but are interested in the fraternal experience.

a. These meet ups would provide a venue for us to interface with Masons already living in the area, and their friends, again forming a relationship with them and making it easier for them to see Masonry as an interesting endeavor.

0. The traveling man, or the Mason passing through, or newly moving into the area is an underserved demographic. There are several corporate headquarters in the Columbia area as well as a proximity to Ft Meade, if we optimize our web presence to be easy to locate and easy to interface with, we can effectively publicize ourselves to the world and capture new members who are already Masons but are new to the area.

0. There are 76 members under 50 that are located within the state of Maryland, these Brothers must be encouraged to replace themselves plus one over the course of the coming decade when we will see a potential cohort of ~43.9% of the membership called from labor.

0. The Brothers between 60 and 68, should be actively asked to talk to their friends and relatives approaching retirement, positioning Masonry as an activity to get them out of their house as a potential source of Masons.

0. The Lodge must let every Brother know that they are entitled to a Masonic memorial service allowing the Lodge the opportunity to show its appreciation to the family of a departed Brother and leave a positive impression on the male relatives who may consider

0.   Retain our existing Brethren by continuing activities that interest them and continue to provide information on Lodge activities to the out of state Brethren to connect them to the Lodge.

0.   Engage in a Facebook marketing campaign to publicize the Lodge in Catonsville, Ellicott City, Columbia to expose potential members to the Lodge. Designed in compliance with the Grand Lodge's guide.

0.   Expand the scholarship program to include Member's children/grandchildren who are entering a graduate program. To gain exposure to additional potential membership.

LONG TERM TACTICS

What are the long-term things the Lodge will do to meet its goals and keep meeting them over time?

If the young Masons can stabilize the membership over the coming decade, it is incumbent on the Lodge to create a stream of candidates from the community that surrounds the Lodge, this is a much longer-term problem and will require consistent effort over the next several Worshipful Masters of Palestine Lodge to effectively execute.

1.   Since the Local Community still has a large cohort of men who are eligible for petitioning the Lodge must be seen in the community and become seen as an active member of the community.
   1.   4th of July Parade
   2.   Chamber of Commerce

0.   Continue with the CHIP program but get the CHIP program at the schools. Partnering with the elementary schools that would put us in front of the families of men who are of potential joining age. This puts the craft in front of them while they are raising their families making them aware of us when they exit their child raising years.

0.   Engaging UMBC's student population, most graduates of the University of Maryland System stay in the state of Maryland and there are some 7,446 undergraduate males and ~1,200 male graduate students.

0.   Open the building - The Holding company and Lodge should work to locate groups that serve the families of our target members and see if the Lodge can be opened to them.

Conclusion

What are our key learnings and how do they inform our strategy and near/long term tactics?

The Catonsville area is a challenging one and will take longer term vision to engage and create a steady stream of candidates from the 21228-zip code. In the short term the younger members must be encouraged to replace themselves to stabilize membership and buy the Lodge time to cultivate a relationship with the greater Catonsville area that provides a stream of candidates. By continued execution of the plan, and changing it as the situation changes, the Lodge can organically sustain itself and avoid membership crunches in the future. I would recommend that the Worshipful Master select a cohort of younger Masons and Past Masters and create a standing committee on long-term membership. It would be recommended that the immediate two Past Master and the Senior and Junior Warden be required committee members to ensure continuity. It would be further recommended that a long-term membership committee be a requirement spelled out in the by-laws to ensure the effort does not get forgotten as leadership changes.

To be effective the membership plan needs to put the candidate first, and match what we can provide (tradition in terms of ritual and fraternalism for example) with their expectations. Not all Masons want to come to Lodge, we need to push Masonry out into the communities that our potential Brothers live and form relationships with them.

Our Strategy

When we talk to the Brethren about what we are trying to do and what we hope to accomplish we want to be able to describe it as succinctly as possible. Here is a statement of the strategy of the ten-year plan in a quick and concise format to create a sense of mission for the brethren:

To successfully attract and retain men in the 21st Century we need to focus on them and how Masonry can align with their goals. This will require the Lodge to practice putting the man first. To succeed and grow we must approach the world, and every man who we meet with two questions:

0.   Whence Came You? - Who is the candidate and where are they coming from?
0.   What Came You Here to Do? - What are their expectations and what are they looking for?

Palestine needs to begin the relationship with a potential new member by focusing on how we can help them find those things by putting them first

As an addendum I have included an addendum of the male population of the town in which my Lodge is located so any of the Brethren reading the plan can see the potential audience for Masonry in the greater Catonsville area.

Addendum: Detailed Catonsville Male Population Analysis

Population In Households In Catonsville	
Total Population:	36,743
Male Population:	17,445
Under 5 years:	1,067
5 to 9 years:	1,078
10 to 14 years:	1,101
15 to 17 years:	726
18 and 19 years:	396
20 years:	254
21 years:	247
22 to 24 years:	706
25 to 29 years:	1,088
30 to 34 years:	1,090
35 to 39 years:	1,015
40 to 44 years:	1,178
45 to 49 years:	1,345
50 to 54 years:	1,455
55 to 59 years:	1,288
60 and 61 years:	409
62 to 64 years:	578
65 and 66 years:	269
67 to 69 years:	363
70 to 74 years:	443
75 to 79 years:	395
80 to 84 years:	433
85 years and over:	521

Sixteen

What do I do now?

Now is the hardest part. You need to do something. It does not need to be perfect, it just needs to be a start. You have looked at your Lodge and you have looked at your Brethren with the hope of being able to come up with a plan that will both engage your Lodge and help it to grow.

Congratulations!

You have learned how to describe your Masonic experience and look at Brothers and men making inquiries and see them for who they are and what they want to achieve through Masonry.

You have done much more than most of your Brethren ever will, and there is still more to do.

Now it is time to grab a calendar and start planning. Lay out your meeting nights and your rehearsals. Now find a copy of your Grand Lodge calendar and mark down the days that the Grand Lodge is having events… look at the calendars of appendant bodies and look at marquis events that would have a large draw of Brothers and mark those on your calendars as well. Finally look at holidays and mark those on your calendar. These are the nights that you are not going to want to schedule things. Let us be realistic: are the Brethren going to be coming to a Lodge event that you scheduled on Mother's Day weekend? It is better to plan around those dates that you are likely not going to see a large turnout than plan something accordingly.

Plan out your events around the time burden that you are already placing on the Brethren. If you meet twice a month and have rehearsals twice a month you likely do not want to pack more than one Lodge function in that month. Look for those months that are not packed with other activities or holidays as your Brothers are going to have multiple commitments. Look at lead-time (or how much time you have before your event) and let your Brethren know what is going on and keep on letting them know. You are going to want to look towards having your volunteers and helpers aligned as far out as possible. If you are going to need to have any ad hoc meetings about an event to align the team, consider doing a conference call, you want to get the Brothers together… but you don't want to burn through the limited cycles that each of your cohort of volunteers have to offer to the Lodge by bringing them out to the Lodge for something that could be done remotely.

Now there is going to come a time when someone new is ready to grab the reins and you need to prepare yourself to see what ideas and enthusiasm that they can bring to this Lodge experience that you share together. Sometimes this is not going to be easy but when you hand over that Oriental chair to the next Brother you need to step out of the way and let them do their best. I had a hard time doing this, so I have made a conscious decision to be the affable sideliner. I don't wear my Past Master's apron or wear my jewel unless there is an event where it is required (I actually purchased a white leather apron that I carry with me when I travel now). I never refer to myself as any Masonic title or office… and I don't discuss anything I did the years I served but I do make a point to call the Master every 60 days or so just to see if there is anything I can help with. I am there to support and give anything I can to the Brothers as they proceed on their Masonic journey.

Seventeen

How do I deal with discouragement?

Masonry is not easy to practice and running a Lodge makes it even harder. You are going to become discouraged from time to time and that is natural. I wish there was something I could say or advice that I could offer that would shield you from that part of the Masonic leadership experience, but I can't and maybe I shouldn't. If we didn't periodically get disappointed it would likely be indicative that we didn't really care that much, and I suppose that if we didn't have an opportunity to question whether something was a success, we wouldn't have tried anything new at all. But it still isn't a pleasant feeling and maybe shielding you from experiencing the pangs of disappointment was the whole reason I put pen to paper... but again I digress. It is my experience that there is a period in the early Summer when each man who is a leader in their Lodge asks themselves why they are doing this. I would pose to you that in the possibility of making your Lodge a success by creating an environment where you are meeting the needs of your Brethren you are given an amazing opportunity: you are given the chance to be the man that you needed when you were a younger man.

What are the requirements to join this gentle craft? You must be a man, be of age, and believe in a higher power. The bar is not that high. Entry is easy for any man who wants it, but entry and practice are two distinctly different things aren't they? Your degrees occur on three nights lasting only a few hours, your catechism maybe another 80 hours... Conversely Masonry is a lifetime practice. Shakespeare can teach us something here. When you are standing wondering whether you are making a difference or longing for the days when there were 800 members at your little country Lodge realize that these sentiments are natural.

For your consideration think of Shakespeare's Henry V, particularly the speech Henry gives on St. Crispin's day. A day where he was facing terrible odds against the French but inspired his men to rise to the occasion:

WESTMORLAND. O that we now had here

But one ten thousand of those men in England

That do no work to-day!

KING. What's he that wishes so?

My cousin, Westmorland? No, my fair cousin;

If we are mark'd to die, we are enough

To do our country loss; and if to live,

The fewer men, the greater share of honour.

God's will! I pray thee, wish not one man more.

By Jove, I am not covetous for gold,

Nor care I who doth feed upon my cost;

It yearns me not if men my garments wear;

Such outward things dwell not in my desires.

But if it be a sin to covet honour,

I am the most offending soul alive.

No, faith, my coz, wish not a man from England.

God's peace! I would not lose so great an honour

As one man more methinks would share from me

For the best hope I have. O, do not wish one more!

Rather proclaim it, Westmorland, through my host,

That he which hath no stomach to this fight,

Let him depart; his passport shall be made,

And crowns for convoy put into his purse;

We would not die in that man's company

That fears his fellowship to die with us.

This day is call'd the feast of Crispian.

He that outlives this day, and comes safe home,

Will stand a tip-toe when this day is nam'd,

And rouse him at the name of Crispian.

He that shall live this day, and see old age,

Will yearly on the vigil feast his neighbours,

And say "To-morrow is Saint Crispian."

Then will he strip his sleeve and show his scars,

And say "These wounds I had on Crispin's day."

Old men forget; yet all shall be forgot,

But he'll remember, with advantages,

What feats he did that day. Then shall our names,

Familiar in his mouth as household words—

Harry the King, Bedford and Exeter,

Warwick and Talbot, Salisbury and Gloucester—

Be in their flowing cups freshly rememb'red.

This story shall the good man teach his son;

And Crispin Crispian shall ne'er go by,

From this day to the ending of the world,

But we in it shall be rememberèd—

We few, we happy few, we band of brothers;

For he to-day that sheds his blood with me

Shall be my brother; be he ne'er so vile,

This day shall gentle his condition;

And gentlemen in England now a-bed

Shall think themselves accurs'd they were not here,

And hold their manhoods cheap whiles any speaks

That fought with us upon Saint Crispin's day.

Shakespeare

King Henry V, Scene III

Why would I include this passage? I included it because Masonry is at a crossroads. The old Masonry is not coming back… but if we few are willing to work for Masonry through Masonry the Brethren will reflect on the work that you have wrought and wish they were there in the quarries with you. Do not lose heart. You are practicing neither speculative or operative but by taking an interest in your Brethren and selflessly working to aid them in their Masonry you are walking a third path and are practicing applied Masonry. Preserving our Craft for a generation of men who have not yet knocked on the preparation room door.

Eighteen

A Word on Degree Capacity

Making Masons is the business of Freemasonry, and the degrees are the vehicle through which we achieve that end. You need to take a hard look at your Lodge's ability to confer the degrees and evaluate whether you need to work on your Lodge's capacity to perform ritual needed to confer the three degrees of ancient Craft Masonry in such a way as to give the candidate an experience that they deserve.

The impact of ritual experience to the candidates and Brothers can't be overstated. Well done ritual is sublime, conversely there is nothing more damaging to a candidate's Masonic experience than being exposed to bad ritual. Your Lodge's ability to perform the work of the degrees has a direct impact on the experience your Brothers receive. If your Lodge struggles to put on its own degrees, you are on a slippery slope as once you lose that ability it is going to be really difficult to get it back. In the old scheme of Lodge management you had a progressive line where men went through each of the chairs in the Lodge room and ended up on the Oriental Chair... along the way they were learning all of the parts necessary to open/close the Lodge and confer the three degrees of ancient Craft Masonry. That does not really happen anymore and due to the reality of our membership numbers and the time required it isn't going to start again any time soon.

Let's think of the progressive line in the 1960's. There were men scrambling to get an officer position, you had a new Master every year! Amazing right? Let's look at it another way, reducing the problem down to the "why" of the men coming into the Lodge. When you had a massive cohort of Brothers passing through degrees annually the proportion of the Brethren who fulfilled their Masonic needs through becoming ritualists is naturally much higher. If 3 out of 60 men raised in 1962 become officers what happens when you only are raising 8 men a year to the Sublime Degree of Master Mason in 2019? Less Masons being raised is yielding less men who are drawn to performing the work. Consider this: If the population of ritualists is smaller now than it has been, Lodges tend to hand a newly raised Master Mason a deacon's staff and a ritual book and then wonder why the man dropped out of the line in a few stations. If men joined Masonry to improve themselves in Masonry, and the ritual is not the vehicle for them to do so what are we doing? I would pose that we are outsourcing the Lodges problem to its new Brothers and thereby robbing those Brothers of the opportunity to in turn improve themselves in Masonry.

So what do we do?
In this thought experiment you could treat the symptoms and make it easier for men to become Master, you could change the degrees to make them less robust. The outcome will improve the number of men becoming Masters.

The outcome would likely be Lodges losing the ability to confer the degrees and candidates receiving a less impressive Masonic experience. Leading to less robust Lodges and Brothers who are more likely to drop membership for non-payment of dues, because if we didn't care enough to make it special for them why would they care enough to send in a dues payment.

Playing the short game will get you a purple apron and a Past Master's jewel. Play the long game and you can build the resilience of your Lodge and ensure that Masonry is existent for the men who are looking for it once you are called from labor.

How?

Look at the three degrees of Masonry as they are being done at your Lodge, think about who is doing what. Sit down and write down the title of each part in each degree. Who in your Lodge knows what part? Take pencil to paper and write out the names of who at your Lodge can perform each part. This may require you to call some of the Past Masters and ask their thoughts.

Once you have a list how many people know each part? What is the age of the Brother who knows of each part?

I ask these questions to help you reframe your reality. Think of putting on the degree like fielding a team. If the progressive line does not function and pushing men into chairs that they are not inspired to take causes issues and only delays the inevitable you need to think of another way, or the Lodge will continue to lose its capacity to confer the degrees. By understanding who knows each part and who can perform it you can look at your Lodge's capacity to do the work dispassionately. Optimally if can you have two people know each part is the goal and if you can ensure that there is someone on hand who can perform the lecture or long parts to every degree you are able to address putting on a degree no matter what the situation with electing a Worshipful Master is, in fact if you are able to look at the entire Lodge's ability to put on a degree you are not suddenly stuck if you don't have a cohort of men coming through the degrees one year. Your Lodge becomes resilient enough to meet the needs of the Brethren no matter what issues you have with petitions or electing leadership, a position that few Lodges are lucky enough to find themselves in.

Let me make the statement to preserve my dues card: my opinions are my own and do not reflect the opinions of any Grand Lodge or appendant body of Freemasonry. That reminder out of the way let me share a view on the degrees of Freemasonry.

What if the Lodge owned the degree work?

I am not suggesting that the Master of the Lodge should not know all the work, but for real resilience the Lodge has to own the work, Let me explain. The degrees of Freemasonry are how we inculcate our lessons and transmit those lessons across generations... and let's be honest many Lodges cannot effectively confer those degrees. If we look at the Lodge's capacity to put on a degree that ensures that even if the progressive line ceases/does not function and the Lodge recycles Past Masters, the Lodge can effectively put on degrees. The capacity to put on all three degrees is critical if the Lodge will operate when there are few candidates coming in and no ritualists amongst those that have been raised. What if we were to look at the lessons of Solomon's Temple for inspiration?

Solomon himself leveraged the Master Architect and his Giblimites to assist in the construction of the Temple. Using these neighbors the Israelites were able to erect the Temple but without them their lack of experience in architecture and monumental architecture in particular likely would have been an insurmountable obstacle. Having challenges with performing the work presents an opportunity to work together with our neighboring Lodges and ask them for help in confer degrees while you look at ways to shore up and grow your Lodge's capacity to perform the work. Consider teaming with another Lodge to provide some of the degree parts that your Lodge cannot fill yourselves. This short-term help is not as easy as asking for some assistance from a degree team but consider that working together builds the strength of two Lodges while utilizing a degree team solves a short-term problem but allows those ritual skills of your Lodge to continue to atrophy. I do not denigrate the skill or commitment of my Brothers who assist in degree teams, but direct observation has stoked my fear that when Lodges use the efforts of these dedicated ritualists… not to meet an emergency need but rather for convenience they, the Lodge, is treating a symptom while exacerbating the root cause. A decade of direct observation leads me to say that this is not an opinion and no mere observation of correlation, this is multi-year study in causation (which writing down likely precludes me from ever attaining any elected Grand Lodge office).

Let's not pull any punches: Lodges that cannot perform the degrees of Freemasonry are in the direst of peril. Look at your entire membership as potential contributors to your degree work if your Lodge is having a challenge filling your officers chairs you need to consider other strategies. A community of friends and Brothers can support your Lodge and aid you in putting on the degrees of Freemasonry effectively providing support and strengthening your

Lodge, build your degree capacity, ask for help from surrounding Lodges, you are not alone… and your candidates are worth it.

Nineteen

They joined, they expressed interest, but they do not show up - Optionality

We, as a fraternity, need to reframe our relationship with time. If I had a dollar for each time, I heard one of my elder Brethren talk about the lack of commitment on the part of young Masons. I would be able to cover my dues for several years (and due to a series of poor life decisions I have filled out many, many petitions). There will always be men who petition the Lodge to try Masonry; there is no level of activity that will engage the man who is not willing to move out of trying Masonry and into committing to practice Masonry so let's look at the Brothers who want to improve themselves in Masonry.

What engages Masons?

Out of the constellation of options that the Brethren have, why what makes your activity compelling enough to attend?

Who is attending things now?

Take a step back and consider for a moment that the largest cohort of Brothers that you see at Lodge events on a regular basis are going to be those Brothers who get their Masonic experience directly by attending Meetings. Hear me out for a moment, I am one of those Brothers... but please do not conflate Lodge attendance with being a good Mason. I would posit that we have been doing that for a century and it is one of the main factors that has led to decreasing membership throughout the same period. Let's deal with some hard truths. Looking through the signs in books throughout the years you will begin to notice a pattern. The number signatures in proportion to total membership show, no matter what the Fraternity may choose to tell itself, that most Masons have never been regular attendees at Lodge. Looking at the sign in books today we see a similar proportion of members attending. This infers that the reason our Lodge rooms were better attended was because instead of seeing 10% to 15% of 200 total members at a meeting the halcyon attendance of the past was a reflection of seating 10% to 15% of 1000 total members. The average attendance simply does not vary that much.

You are not going to change that, I am not going to change that, no Grand Lodge program is going to change that. The simple truth is that there are only a set cohort of Brothers who achieve their Masonic experience by regularly attending Lodge meetings. If we are seeing a decrease in membership across the board but we are still seeing the ratio of attendees hold firm what does that suggest? Could we be reaching the replacement rate for men who are receiving their Masonic experience via our meetings? If we are in fact reaching equilibrium in the membership for regular Lodge attendees what would that mean for the Craft?

I would posit that it confirms the pattern that we are seeing now. In a world where the Fraternity is optimized around the Lodge room, I would expect to see the number of Masons whose "why" is realized in something other than the Lodge Room i.e. the ritual or a meeting to steadily decrease and men opt out after they realize that the Masonry that they were looking for is not found in the Masonry we are providing. That thesis, my Brothers, is confirmed for me by the reality of the increasing rates of non-payments of dues that we see and the churn rates one, three, and five years after joining the craft.

We are optimized around the Lodge room.

We focus our activities on the Lodge room, we train our leaders around the Lodge room, our leadership is composed of Masons whose "why" is fulfilled in the Lodge room. Attend a Grand Lodge meeting and see the chart of decreasing membership and increasing rates of Non-payment of dues and then go back and read the sign-in books comparing them to the membership rolls. You are going to find that the data infers that most Masons do not get the Masonic experience that they joined seeking by immersion in the Lodge room once they receive their three degrees nor are new men who are seeking the craft found in the Lodge room.

Let's look at the problem holistically:

In prior eras this was frankly not a problem. The appendant bodies were able to absorb the Brothers whose Masonic "why" fell outside of the stated or called Blue Lodge meeting. But that cycle is broken because in order for it to function there has to be a steady volume of men being raised and seeking further light in Masonry. The appendant bodies as vehicles for Masonic experience is dependent on a large volume of men coming through the Blue Lodge. You have seen evidence in your feedback from your Lodge Brothers men joining our Craft for a plurality of reasons so there should always be some group of men whose "why" was Masonic leadership, management, or ritual. If the volume is large enough not all men would have been able to meet their Masonic needs through Blue Lodge leadership. In this case logic would hold that the steady stream of men coming into the Blue Lodge in the golden age would find it in other Masonic Bodies, effectively achieving their Masonic experience while providing a vital need. These Brothers would provide the support and leadership function and confer degrees. This cycle breaks down when the overall number of men going through the Blue Lodge falls. Why? Because those men who would seek to realize their Masonic leadership, management, or ritual needs would by necessity remain in the Blue Lodge where the opportunity abounds. You may not agree with my thesis, but to you who disagree with me I have one question. I ask you honestly how many officers and leaders in our Craft do you see at every meeting and are leaders in every Masonic body in your jurisdiction?

The first step in fixing a problem is acknowledging the problem and I pose that we do not have a membership problem.

Let me explain.

If we have optimized the fraternity for the experience of those Brothers who fulfill their Masonic "why" through Blue Lodge meetings, how do the 85% to

90% of the Brethren who are not in the Lodge room regularly receive their Masonic experience?

Let us examine. We can agree that when the ecosystem of Masonry was fully functional the appendant bodies provided some of the Brethren their Masonic experience and helped them achieve their Masonic "why" but looking at the historic membership of the appendant bodies not every Blue Lodge Mason was a member of an appendant body and not all of the members of the individual bodies were regular attendees of either their Blue Lodge or the appendant body. This infers to me that the ~10% to ~15% ratio of attendees holds and the Brothers attending their appendant bodies regularly are the same Brothers who are active in their Blue Lodge. What the earlier system provided exceptionally well when operating at optimal efficiency was optionality. By optionality I mean that it created a system of activities and events that provided a wealth of options for members to get together. And that optionality provided the context for the Brethren to come together and experience pure Masonic Education. The challenge with our current state of affairs is that in a world where there are fewer and fewer Brothers whose Masonic "why" is fulfilled through Masonic leadership and ritual, our demands on those who do achieve their Masonic experience through these vital roles are untenable. In the prior era optionality created a system where men could find their Masonic "why" but if our present-day era is optimized too heavily for the Lodge room we are only catering to a subset of the Craft and only addressing a small portion of the total available market. So how can we collectively be surprised by our membership numbers and our losses to non-payment of dues?

So what can you do?

Don't lose heart!

The 21st Century calls for another variation of optionality which provides you a tremendous opportunity. A 30-year-old who petitions today will go through multiple life phases throughout their time in the Masons. They may get married, they may have children, they may take care of a parent, they may need to focus on a career. If the Lodge seeks to compete for a Brother's attention any attempt to take the limited time which he has available from his young wife, or his children is a losing proposition. Success is reliant on creating opportunities for Brothers to participate not where we need them in Masonry but by providing a Masonry that puts them where they need to be. To give them an option to spend time with their Brothers in a way that does not have them out of the house for five hours on a Thursday night every other week. Consider on-ramps and off ramps in your long-term planning. What activities can you plan around the Brothers who are focused on being amazing Fathers but really believe there is value in Masonry? Addressing a Brothers "why" around their life stage transforms the Lodge from another commitment to a release valve... a veritable safe harbor where the wicked cease from troubling and the weary shall find rest.

Whatever you do, please resist the temptation to compile a list of all the Brothers who are not attending Lodge and individually calling them to ask them, "What can we do to get you back in Lodge?" Their Masonic experience may not be fulfilled through regular meetings, or their life phase may preclude attendance for the time being. Our role at the Blue Lodge is to make Masons and if we do so through Masonry, catering to the motivations of the Brethren and serving the culture of the Lodge, we can engage all of our Brothers. And it is only by engaging the Masonic experience of all the Brethren that we can hold onto the silent majority of Masonry.

Twenty

But I need help right now!

There are no easy answers and there are Lodges that are in crisis now. These Lodges may be several steps away from being able to use the strategies and tactics in the preceding chapters. I appreciate your challenge and would like to offer up some interim tactics to help you help your Lodge. Like all good stories let's jump in at the beginning.

Maybe your Lodge has barely enough guys to open with minimal attendance.

Maybe you just came into Masonry, and you are excited, but the lack of engagement has discouraged you.

Maybe you believe in your Lodge enough to make it a little better than you found it.

We are going to fake it until we make it.

1.) Travel to visit local Lodges, invite your Brothers. When you visit these Lodges invite the Brethren you are visiting to your Lodge.

2.) Start a Lodge Instagram account – Because this allows you to capture experiences that men who are looking for the craft want (fellowship, tradition, esprit de corps) without any of the burden of administering a Facebook wall or a larger website. Create a tag with your Lodge and a tag with your town and Masons i.e. #yourtownMasons

3.) Take candid shots of younger Brethren doing cool things whenever you are together, post those candid shots to Instagram and tag them with Masonic tags. Under no circumstances post masonic memes or trivia. You want to create the appearance of activity so that a man who is seeing the pictures can see themselves in your Lodge. Memes and trivia are not a good look for anybody.

4.) Make a simple webpage as a landing page. Only publish your address, your meeting nights, a photo of your Lodge and a link to your Instagram account. This will allow a man who is looking for Masonry to see that your Lodge exists and jump directly to Instagram where they see young Masons doing cool things.

5.) Get together with your friends regularly, invite your Brothers, remembering step three. Treat any opportunity to get two Masons together as a Masonic activity not every activity needs to be a festive board... you, a guy from your Lodge, and a friend going to a baseball game is a Masonic activity if there are Masons there, right? When you take a shot of the three of you and post it to Instagram the guy researching Masonry is not going to know the percentage of Masons in any picture, they are just going to see a group of guys having fun (and want to be part of that).

6.) Repeat.

These six steps will give your Lodge the appearance of activity and will get a cadence of activities together to slowly build momentum until you are able to reach a critical mass of potential attendees to start planning things.

When you see events that might be cool at neighboring Lodges go. Invite the younger Brothers out or drag them along. The means are less important than the ends. Work to provide your Brothers with an awesome Masonic experience by leveraging the hard work of surrounding Lodges.

I am going to apologize in advance, but you cannot finesse degree work. There is no that there... but seriously this ritual is the vehicle for our lessons, so you are going to need a strategy to ensure your Brothers get a memorable experience.

Try colonizing your degree work. You visited neighboring Lodges. During your travels you likely will see degree work that will impress. Meet the Masons whose degree work impresses you. Ask those men to help you with yours.

Schedule regular rehearsals and build up your proficiency in the degree work.

If you are in a pinch, ask your Grand Lodge or a degree team for help.

Have fun because if you are your Brothers will too and their fun will yield dividends.

Twenty-One

Final Thoughts

I love the Craft, and if you made it to this point you do too. If you are willing to do a little bit of work, then you can improve your Lodge. If you concentrate on the best experience for the Brothers, then you can improve their Masonic experience. Look for ways to make every interaction that you have with the Brethren for little ways to make it special for them.

There is a Japanese idea called kaizen which means something to the effect of change for the better or continuous improvement. This is a philosophy that looks to improvement not as an epiphany but rather a gradual process that methodically looks to improve. What would your Lodge look like if every meeting you sought to be 1% better than the meeting before? That type of slow change is within your grasp, and you can make it happen if you look at your Lodge's culture and the 'why's' of you Brothers. Masonry is sublime and your efforts can make your Lodge some of your Brethren's fondest memories.

Afterward

This is a call to action, so hold onto your seats as I try to hold onto my dues cards.

The early chapters of this text are dedicated to finding the culture of your Lodge, the why of your members, and plotting a pathway to help your Brothers improve themselves in Masonry by taking the demographics of your community into account and designing the Masonry you want around your reality. This text is just a start and I hope that the tactics and strategies help you make your, and by extension your Brothers', Lodge experience better. I believe that your efforts, and those of the Brethren that you inspire, can ensure that Freemasonry is available for men into the next century. The truth of the matter is that a Lodge renaissance will take work and your success is predicated on your Lodge's resilience to meet the challenges today and withstand those that will arise in the future.

Your Lodge is part of a larger ecosystem of Freemasonry which is a Macro-problem and what are you going to do about that?

Looking at the business problem of Freemasonry the conclusion that I have reached is that while we cannot predict the future we can prepare for its uncertainty. This missive is an outline on how to approach uncertainty with resilience.

Let me preface my words with a statement of principles:

1. I love Freemasonry, it has given me far more than I have ever dedicated to it.
2. I believe that we Masons of today owe our elder Brethren who preserved the craft for future generations deserve a tremendous debt of gratitude for laboring often unsung to preserve Masonry when there was nobody knocking on the West Gate.
3. I believe that there is dignity in all work.

4. My opinions are strictly my own and do not represent the views of any Grand Lodge, Lodge, or subordinate body of Freemasonry, so please do not take my dues card(s).

There are big problems confronting our world and these 'Macro' challenges can be directly translated to the Microcosms of your Lodge. Let's focus on the challenges that Masonry can aid the world in: Masonry can provide a man with a place where he can develop parts of himself amongst men who are only interested in his success as opposed to the stark isolation of the modern world. As a Mason he does not labor alone; his Brothers invest in him to help him achieve his why. In many ways each Mason is a supporting character in every other Brother's Coelho Esque[6] personal legend and through the journey, through the process, he masters his craft… by helping his Brothers master themselves. I apologize for my digression but let us agree that problems (even these problems) are not insurmountable, and that Masonry has real value in the lives of men.

Let's adjust our mindset to look forward.

One of Maryland's Past Grand Masters was fond of a Charles Kettering quote: "My interest is in the future because I am going to spend the rest of my life there." It is apt, the craft needs to look not at what Masonry was but what Masonry could be because frankly if we pine for the past, we sell our future short.

What would you want to achieve if money was not an object?

What would you want to achieve if time was not an object?

---

[6] Paulo Coelho is a Brazilian author of the book the Alchemist. The Alchemist tells the story of a shepherd boy named Santiago. Believing a dream to a call to action he seeks out a fortune teller who explains the dream as meaning he will discover a treasure at the pyramids of Egypt. Early in the tale he meets Melchizedek the king of Salem and introduces the concept of a Personal Legend. Your Personal Legend "is what you have always wanted to accomplish. Everyone, when they are young, knows what their Personal Legend is. Read this book for its application of personal Masonry.

Consider your Lodge… what if all that Masonry wanted to achieve was not bound by time or finance?

You are going to have to be willing to open yourself to approach the problems confronting your Lodge differently than you have in the past. Think of the conversations you have had about Masonry, the meetings you have attended at your Grand Lodge… odds are likely backward facing. Meaning all of that talking about decreases in membership and how we need to perform x, y, or z to turn the tide. Look at it probabilistically for a moment… What are the odds that any single program is going to encapsulate all the factors that are required to turn the ship of Masonry around? Would you take those odds? The task may seem huge. In my own jurisdiction we have ~12k Brothers as of this publication the average age of which is in the mid-sixties, the typical mortality age in the US is in the mid ~70's for men… add in the NPD numbers and membership will be halved over the next 5-10 years.

I am not a pessimist, and you should not be either.

You could have faith that it will all work out for Masonry; you could hope that it all works out for Masonry. Or you can practice Charity.

Let me quote the text of General Ahiman Rezon, by Daniel Sickels, [1868]: "The greatest of these is CHARITY: for our faith may be lost in sight; hope ends in fruition; but charity extends beyond the grave, through the boundless realms of eternity." This idea of charity is derived from the Latin concept of Caritas which was a deep caring for our fellow man. The earlier part of this book talked about how we can practice charity and talk to our Brothers about the Lodge they want, their "why" for joining Masonry, and work together to bring a Masonic experience to fruition. Widen your gaze… consider that Masonry will be here after we have been called from labor and the Lodge gives each of the Brothers who call it their own a chance to change the lives of men that have not even been born yet for the better.

Time is on your side.

You do not need to accomplish your personal Masonic journey in a year, you have a lifetime. In the same vein you can look at the challenges ahead for your Lodge and break them into a smaller piece because time is not an object.

You may retort, my Lodge is struggling. We need help today. To you I say leverage the tools listed earlier in this text and consider how you can set up your Lodge to continue to meet the needs of your Brothers. Each Lodge has its own culture, resides in a community with unique dynamics, and is made up of men bringing their own talents to the endeavor. No one program will ever suffice in meeting the unique needs of your Lodge but utilizing tools we can build something and adapt to the needs of tomorrow.

Let us consider how to approach the problem by addressing two generalizations:

- When we as a Fraternity talk about Freemasonry, we generally approach it in terms of membership. What if that was the wrong approach?
- When we look at finances in Freemasonry, we generally approach them in terms of a retiree working not to outlive their principle. What if the craft did not consider itself constrained by time?

Let us start with the membership question.

There is a business maxim that we roll out like a banal platitude: That which is measured gets done. The catch twenty-two of the business world is that most maxims are applied like a panacea... by business people who are grasping at the idea and passionately believe if we determine this one root cause we can solve the problem. Look at Wells Fargo. Wells Fargo at the turn of the century had one key metric after revenue: cross selling. They were looking to increase the total types of services that customers utilized from the bank to capture as much of the customer's spend as possible. Great for the customers who need the services, great for the bank's revenue, and great for the shareholders... but there was a problem. This population of existing customers is finite and there was a series of events that had to happen for someone to become a new customer. Someone would have to come to the bank to open a new account and be opened to expand their engagement. Because this cross-selling number was THE NUMBER that staff was judged on they were signing up family and friends, they were pressuring savings account holders to open checking accounts, and looking to offer credit cards to mortgage holders... sadly some staff were signing up customers for accounts without their knowledge. This caused a huge backlash where the media exposed the malfeasance and executives lost their jobs.

How did the Wells Fargo story make you feel?

My heart goes out to the line employees who were given one metric they were being measured against. Imagine starting every day with a staff meeting where you are asked how many accounts you were going to open. Sure that is how a sales organization works but there is a subtle difference here. In every meeting from the Shareholders to the stock analysts from the C suite to the bank branch was focused on one number: new accounts. The measurement of this single number drove the behavior of the bank's employees for good or ill.

Let us pivot back to Masonry.

How many meetings have you been in where membership comes up? Meetings where the falling numbers are projected on a screen and the assembled Brothers are deflated by them. This is paired with a big idea that is going to turn it all around, we then elect new leaders and repeat the whole process again.

How does your Lodge talk about membership?

How many Grand Lodge meetings have you attended where a chart of declining membership is shown?

If all we talk about is membership, what impact does that have on our behavior?

It has been my experience that we do talk about guarding the west gate and quality over quantity and we do that at every level of the fraternity. But at the same time we are focusing on a single metric: Membership.

What is the impact?

We have men dropping for non-payment of dues, we have men who do not fit catechism, we continue to have shrinking membership rolls.

Something is profoundly broken, and my thesis is that our focus is the Lodge room instead of the holistic Masonic experience.

Have you spoken candidly to men who fail to advance or people who opt to go NPD?

I have called the Brothers who went NPD from my Lodge for a decade, and I learned much.

The Brothers who I have called regarding NPD's. Those Brothers who have opted to just not pay their dues any longer describe Masonry in two forms: either not being what they expected or not delivering. Even with the hundreds of men who opt to just not come back on an annual basis it is highly probable that the couple dozen conversations I have had over the past few years are representative of the problem. We are not good at mapping that inherent motivation of the man to the culture and norms of our Lodges, and we are replicating this problem at scale.

So how do we fix it?

Let's look at the business problem another way. Please indulge my veering off for a moment, it will all come together I promise you.

I love Netflix. I can stream a documentary about the building of the pyramids on my phone at 3am while on a business trip to Fargo, but how did Netflix get there and what can the craft learn from the corporate world?

I focus on Netflix because examining the company as the incremental steps that lead to from the theater to streaming video can illustrate what led us to this point in the Craft's trajectory and how we can capitalize on the future. I bring this up because the Craft is at a fulcrum point and has been for nearly a century now... and there has never been a more opportune time to leverage the structure of Masonry to meet the needs of two generations of men.

Look at the Golden age of fraternalism, a period when there were hundreds of fraternal organizations and one in three men were members in a fraternal organization. What gave rise to this development and what were these fraternal organizations? Let's split fraternities into two camps: benefit organizations and mystery organizations. The benefit organizations allowed members to join multiple organizations assembling a portfolio of services while being part of a community. For example I could join the Odd Fellows and protect my family via their death benefit and could also become one of the Independent Foresters and enjoy the peace of mind provided by their Insurance... creating a comprehensive and valuable group of services. I could join the Masons for the cachet of the mystery work and enjoy access to a wide section of men of different social stations (should they elect to accept my petition). This Golden age also saw the creation of organizations like the Mayflower Society or the D.A.R. (Daughters of the American Revolution) where membership was limited to those with the right pedigree and signaled virtue by means of familial ties.

The benefit societies began to fold as they were gradually replaced with access to corporate insurance and state sponsored government programs arose and effectively outcompeted the offerings of the Fraternal organizations. The collapse of the benefit branch of the fraternal movement created a vacuum in fraternalism to the benefit of the mystery fraternities. It is no surprise that the downturn of the benefit organizations corresponds with the beginning of peak membership of Freemasonry. With Lodges located in communities across the country men seeking a fraternal experience were able to find both convenient locations and a plurality of options for additional fellowship, provided via the appendant bodies for those men who were accepted into the gentle Craft. This volume of men seeking a fraternal experience provided Lodges an influx of dues dollars which subsidized this premium experience. Like a $0.50 movie ticket buying the patron access to a multimillion-dollar production the dues at the Blue Lodge purchased access to a premium experience and a selective association of men at a budget price. During this period, the member has low dues and a plurality of options in terms of their fraternal experience through the variety found within the appendant bodies of Freemasonry. The high watermark of membership was a period where Lodges cannot confer degrees fast enough and everyone wanted to be an officer... but if we look to adjacent organizations i.e. the animal organizations (Elks or Moose) or mission centric organizations (Rotary or Kiwanis) we see a hint of a change coming.

During the Golden Age of fraternalism flatter organizations began to arise where the central purpose that brought men together was optimized and everything that did not add to that part of the experience was excised, think the Moose for fun and the Rotary for business networking. These organizations experienced a membership boom-let like the Masons in conjunction with the expansion of the suburbs in the post-war period. Think of this class of organizations like the ability to rent a video at Blockbuster; these flat organizations allowed the member to consume just what they wanted and nothing that they didn't. The animal organizations in particular with their clubhouses cut out the biweekly Lodge meeting with its business and degree work and allowed the average Moose to only consume the fraternal togetherness as little or as often as he wanted on his own schedule. Our Masonic Lodges, our Chapters and our Shrine Temples didn't provide this same variety of options without the business and degree overhead inherent to the Masonic system.

The rise of convenience consumption which I liken to being able to go to the grocery or to do one stop shopping at a department store. People were becoming acculturated to buying the ease and convenience of getting exactly what they wanted when they wanted it. To the mid twentieth century man

Masonry with its experiences on set schedules is not conducive to the convenience consumption model. Men could still be interested in fraternalism, but the majority were interested in consuming that convenience in a convenience model. I pose to you that the accelerated membership decline over the past fifty years has a direct correlation to our inability to cater to convenience consumption that Boomers grew up to expect. Instead of a Blockbuster model where a man could take what he wanted when he wanted it the Fraternity by its nature is locked delivering a meeting-based experience at specific places and times.

Push this generation forward. The 21st century fraternal problem is that we have two generations of men: Millennials and Gen Z who value experience over material goods. This shift in values should be great for the Craft but the challenge will be that these generations are used to consuming their experience anywhere and anytime a la Hulu or Netflix. How can Freemasonry capitalize on the experience focus of these next generations? I fear that our organization will focus on efforts to streamline and pare down the Masonic experience… yielding to the siren song of making Masonry easier. This would be a profoundly shortsighted answer, in our present age men can consume their content anywhere, at any time, on any device and this age of extreme flexibility is the greatest ally of the Craft. If men of these latest generations value experience above material possessions and if they are able to consume everything from movies to college classes on demand our weakness of set meetings in set buildings at set times becomes a differentiator when combined with the experience of Masonry. The caveat, and it is a major caveat, is the experience.

Let me put is plainly: If Freemasons collectively are focusing on raw membership numbers as the single indicator of organizational success and the Craft has been optimized organizationally to deliver an experienced tailored to the Brethren who receive their Masonic experience via the experience of coming to Lodge meetings, but only 10-15% of Masons address their Masonic why by attending Lodge meetings. Then is it any wonder why membership gains are offset by attrition via non-payment of dues when what we are delivering is not now nor has it ever been compelling to ~85% to ~90% of our members.

So what can we do?

We can focus on your Lodge and how it caters to the needs of the Brethren.

If you leverage some of the tools… we have mapped out a way that you can make a difference in your Lodge. You can work to engage the silent majority of the Brethren whose Masonic why is not inextricably linked to Lodge meetings. Looking back in the text we talked about how many Brothers we need to sustain our Lodge. If we need to have 4 Brothers join a year to continue to be able to work as a Lodge that is a way easier number to achieve than a replacement number of 3,000 Brothers across the jurisdiction.

Let us talk about why your Lodge is key to the continual viability of the craft in the present century.

There are three problems that keep me up at night when it comes to the Craft:

1. What happens when regularized annual returns and the power of compound interest's future performance does not meet expectations?
2. How does the application of business thinking impact the craft?
3. What is the mission of Masonry?

This may seem to be a hard pivot from our earlier conversation on the Lodge specifically but bear with me because it has direct application to your Lodge

The world is chasing returns and if you have looked at your portfolio there seem to be fewer and fewer easy dollars available. Business is cyclical, and past performance is no indication of future performance… But what happens when we no longer see strong year over year growth? For me that isn't a big deal as I don't want to convert my securities to cash for decades but if you were a person in retirement reliant on dividends and sales of securities you may have to change your retirement plans. I am acutely nervous about the emergence of slim returns. How will Grand Lodge's operate their businesses when they have continued diminishing dues dollars and the returns on their investments are no longer predictable?

The dues are problematic but the gross number of dues paying members, not income, gives me pause at a jurisdictional level. Decreased numbers of Masons equate to fewer bequests and charitable donations in the future to the Grand Lodge which could then lead to an accelerated consumption of investment principle. This in turn could lead the craft to dip into the principle as opposed to the interest of centuries of the gifts of our departed Brethren to continue to prop up operating expenses and charities further diminishing the long-term viability of the organization and making the problem more acute.

This is the point where you dear reader may say Charles you do not know what you are talking about. I appreciate your position but hear me out. I want you to consider two scenarios:

> Have you ever talked to a college student who signed up for their first credit card and got themselves in a little trouble spending more than they had?

> Have you ever talked to a person who took a little money to Vegas or Atlantic City and lost it at the tables and then doubled down hoping to win it all back and ended up losing that cash as well?

Consider the downturns that have occurred in the marketplace during the .com burst of the turn of the century, the great recession, and the COVID-19 collapse. Next time you go to your Grand Lodge ask them if they have a financial report, what percentage of current operating budgets are being subsidized by endowments? Let me ask you again, what do you think happens if a once in a lifetime interruption of regular returns takes place (like the three I have seen since I have entered the workforce)? Add variables such as stagflation, Japonesque lost decades, and politicized monetary policy and you can see why this keeps me up at night.

What actions could be taken to shore up the financial position? What business thought could we apply to the problem?

As we see more of our elder Brethren be called from labor, we lose more than their friendship; we lose the connection that we had with their families. If fewer boomers joined the craft than men in the silent and greatest generation(s) the probability of millennials having a father or grandfather who was a Mason is diminished so who will inspire them to join? If the general decrease of the percentage of the population that are Masons requires the craft to make the population aware of the mission and values of the craft. PR and Communications are critical to the long-term sustainability of the fraternity because people need to know that we exist. Diminishing returns from the soft connections that Masonry had in our communities is a critical loss.

Ask yourself if we could accelerate the acquisition of members through awareness how we could confer degrees on the petitioners? The Craft could enact policies to hasten progress through degrees such as doing away with catechism requirements, we could adjust the degrees to make them easier to put on: *but to what effect*?

Let us perform another thought experiment:

Supposition: What would the impact of 2,000 hypothetical petitioners be across 110 hypothetical Lodges?

Question: Could the Lodges perform the work?

Practical solution: Some, but not all, Lodges would be able to absorb the EAs, so we could do one day classes or coordinate degree teams.

Supposition: Do we have enough catechism instructors to teach 2,000 men going through the degrees?

Question: What if they did not need the formal catechism to advance?

Practical solution: Decrease or remove the catechism requirement.

So we hypothetically have a pathway to absorb the 2,000 men. The problem with this hypothetical is that many jurisdictions have done these exact things and it has had negligible impact on membership because progress in membership gains is negated by non-payment of dues on the backend.

You could conclude that Masonry does not have a problem with petitions, it has a retention problem and that would be an adjacent issue but is not the root. I pose to you that Freemasonry has a connection problem that is exacerbated as we increase the volume of candidates moving through the degrees because the system is set up to deliver a Masonic experience that only fulfills the needs of ~10 – 15% of masons.

This churn exposes another cost, the acquisition cost of those actual members. How much did it cost to get each petition and how many years do they need to be a dues paying member with assessments flowing to the Grand Body prior to even breaking even? You can do the back of the napkin math X represents the total amount spent on membership acquisition in your jurisdiction. Y represents the total number of inquiries generated from that effort or $X/Y =$ the cost per inquiry. Not every inquiry leads to a petition so let us take it one step further how many petitions were generated from the effort. Let's assign this variable as P. Dividing the total amount of dollars spent on membership acquisition X by the total number of petitions P gives us the cost per petition. Now we can look at the magic number of the breakeven period. What is your Grand Lodge assessment? Let us assign the annual amount that your lodge pays to the Grand Lodge a variable A and then divide the cost per petition or P giving us $A/P =$ the breakeven period. This is the number of years required for the Brother to remain active in the fraternity for the Craft not to lose money on the engagement. In order to not lose money we can't lose our Brother as

NPD's. But to do so we also need to be sticky to our membership, which requires speaking to their personal Masonic why.

My jurisdiction's communications and awareness programs have done a superb job attracting interest. The challenge is that using factory production as an analogy we have a surplus of raw material that we are not adequately able to process, this drives up the cost of goods because we have an artificially high fallout from our process in the form of NPD's.

In our thought experiment designed to accelerate the acquisition of members, what component was missing from the equation? I would posit that it is the Masonic experience that was missing. Let us look at it another way. Consider the experience that you have had with your Mother Lodge. The men you have met, the stories that you have shared. The laughs that have arisen from an errant word in the ritual or the sadness that lingered after a Masonic memorial service. Those things were all predicated by your relationship with the Brethren and how did you develop those relationships? You developed them by being amongst the Brethren which in turn where you are exposed mouth to ear to how men actually applied Masonry in their daily lives.

The success of your Lodge will be determined by the experience that you give the Brother, the opportunities that you give him to achieve what he came to do in Masonry (by speaking to his why).

Even an influx of bodies would not fix the problem because the scale of the membership acquisition needed to offset the consumption of endowment dollars in our hypothetical scenario could not be absorbed. I fear the answer is an unpleasant one, you must run the organization like a business, or more specifically a mission based non-profit. Use zero-based budgeting and anything that does not support the mission of the organization does not get funded. Privatize or spin-off anything that does not support the mission.

So what is the mission of Masonry? We invest in men, they come to us looking for something and we help them be the men they aspired to be. The pathway is different for each Mason, but if we do the work of Masonry in our Lodges our Brothers become the types of men the world needs them to be.

Those are nice words Matulewicz but how do we get there? By setting up your Lodge for success not ten years out, but realizing you are just a steward of Masonry for men who have not even been born yet… a century out.

A Simple Plan – Ensuring the Next Century

We as Masons must commit to relentlessly drive individual lodge experience across time. Realizing that we do not need to increase membership in the short term we need to preserve the craft for next century. What does this line of thinking yield? If we invest in the local Blue Lodges, we create a system that is resilient enough to outlast shocks to the system. Lodges that focus on experience speak specifically to the why of its members which in turn creates lasting bonds with its membership. The Lodge that engages Brothers retains Brothers. And it begins by having Lodges change their relationship with membership.

Consider the conversation on membership. If we assume the Fraternity has the capacity to exist in the next century, we should manage our Lodge's as if our timeline is a century out, not one Master's term. In turn we should widen the scope of our consideration of membership.

In a world where our organization can last for centuries but our membership numbers display variation in the short term, how does a hypothetical Lodge determine the health of its aggregate membership? Three metrics can be borrowed from the business world and applied to looking at the broader century view of your Lodge.

Average Customer Value

Average Customer Lifespan

Customer Lifetime Value

What are these numbers about?

We want to understand the Average customer value which in business is formulated as average purchase price divided by average purchase frequency rate. In our exercise let us divide the average dues divided by the average number of years a man is paying his dues. This will give us a feel for the total number of dollars that the Lodge can expect to yield from a member who is being engaged and fulfilled by his local Lodge or the average member value.

The next factor we would want to calculate is the average customer's lifetime span. This can be calculated by looking at the sum of customer lifespans divided by the total number of customers. This would also be adjusted slightly for the purposes of Masonry; we would be able to substitute the variables where we would look at the average amount of time a man is a Mason and divide this by the total membership of your hypothetical jurisdiction. This would tell us the average amount of time a Brother is engaged in Masonry or the average member lifespan.

The final factor is the number we would want in the front of mind because it is the most vital: The customer's lifetime value. This is calculated by taking the customer value and multiplying it by the average customer lifespan. For our purposes we would take the average member value and multiply it by the average member lifespan. This calculation provides the total lifetime value of a member.

Let's widen our gaze to the Fraternity as a whole. If the current situation across the fraternity has any improvements made in volume of petitions acquired negated by the number of Brothers being called from labor or opting to be dropped for non-payment of dues it does not matter how much progress is made in a funnel of membership. Abstracting the fraternity down to a business shows the business Masonry is in is not transactional Masonry is using the lens of business a subscription. Looking at successful Software as a Service companies we learn that their business model is not to sell you a one time license, rather they convert the capital expense of enterprise software to an operational expense of an annual subscription. The Grand Lodges have their annual assessments that they charge their constituent Lodges per member, they are essentially charging a per member license for Masonry. Like downward price pressure in the software space Grand Lodge's often have their assessments specifically dictated in their constitutions making dynamic price increases highly unlikely, this applies equally to your dues.

The inability to change price structure and the recurring nature of assessments leave the Craft few options.

So what do we do?

If we collectively have not found near term success in increasing our membership in the past century, we need to use time differently. Time is our greatest asset, and we focus on the long game of lifetime member value and have that inform our behaviors.

If there is a potential for irregular rates of return on endowments and there is also decreasing membership the most important thing that Lodges can measure is the average value of members over their lifetime. Managing member experience to increase retention can be impacted directly by investing in the constituent Lodges. Since every Lodge has a unique culture, a unique set of talents and resources, as well as their own sets of challenges this creates an environment where any program or plan applied at a jurisdictional level will yield average results as the intended results will only be meeting the needs of a subset of members in a subset of Lodges.

There are Lodges with highly engaged memberships. Looking at the average engagement or the average Brothers at a Lodge event divided by the total membership the data would highlight those Lodges which are most engaging their Brethren. If we were to look at the three earlier numbers culminating in the lifetime value of a member for these Lodges a jurisdiction would be able to highlight those Lodges that are both engaging Brothers and creating profitable relationships for the governing body. Identifying those Brothers who are contributing to the success of these optimally performing Lodges the governing body could parse who is contributing their talents and what those talents are. Qualifying and categorizing these talents across a spectrum the governing body could engage these potential change agents to help Lodges that want help with ideas or implementation of programs that align with the unique culture and mores of the Lodge. Strategic deployment of aid to meet the needs of individual Lodges would create Lodges that engage their Brothers and engaged Brothers are Brothers who feel connected enough to continue to pay their dues. Brothers who feel connected are Masonry in action and carry their Masonry into their lives and that Masonry in action.

Imagine a world where the communications and outreach efforts of jurisdictions are filtered through to optimally performing Lodges. Lodges that are engaging and retaining members. What happens to NPD numbers? Organically they would decrease over time and the lifetime member value to the Lodges would increase. How different would our world look if we had a few more men who wanted to be better living lives in their communities? Since there are no new Masons in Lodge rooms what type of virtuous membership cycle would be created if the efforts out outreach and advertising were strictly supplemental to the acquisition of members by example?

Where do the appendant bodies fit into all of this? There are those in the Craft who feel that the other bodies are distractions from the dire needs of Ancient Craft Masonry. I cannot agree. A Masonic jurisdiction is an ecosystem, and its component parts perform a vital task. The youth groups provide services to children, but they also serve to keep men who are motivated to focus on their families an opportunity to meet that need while remaining engaged with the Craft meeting their need of being a good parent. The Shrine, Tall Cedars, and the York and Scottish Rites have a harder value proposition as the call of the world's greatest charity or being the playground of Masonry or even a vehicle to receive further light becomes less compelling as there are less members who would naturally be drawn to their missions. Both they and the Blue Lodge's would be best served by pooling resources and efforts creating a virtuous cycle where appendant bodies are able to scale by leveraging the entire memberships of groups of Lodges. The Lodges benefit by participating in events of a scale and scope unseen since the Halcyon days of distant memory and the appendant bodies gain access to larger groups of Masons for longer. Were a jurisdiction to operate like an ecosystem all of its component parts would enter into coopetition[7] where each player in this ecosystem works to not only do what is best for their own piece of Masonry but also works in the best interest of each of the other parts which is the underlying Masonic experience of the Brethren.

The plan to preserve Masonry for the next century begins with each Lodge, the relentless and unapologetic focus on delivering on the culture of each Lodge. If young men value experience above all else and the entertainment options that we see ourselves as competing against can be consumed anytime anywhere then young men have never had more power to reorganize their entertainment consumption to accommodate real and deep experience. There are very few organizations that can deliver real and deep experiences left in the world save one that has a footprint in nearly every town and has been wringing its hands over membership numbers for half a century. Masonry can meet the needs of its target audience and thrive through doing nothing more complicated than delivering Masonry. That proposition requires preparing each Lodge to be resilient enough to succeed for their next 100 years. Building those three numbers into your Lodge planning creates a level of resiliency and a level of resiliency ensures that your Lodge will be there many years from now when next centuries men knock on the West Gate.

Let us all look to the most integral part of Masonry, the Masonic experience without which there is no growth nor retention.

Thank you for helping to preserve Masonry for the next generation.

---

[7] Coopetition or co-opetition is a neologism coined to describe cooperative competition. Coopetition is a portmanteau of cooperation and competition. Basic principles of co-opetitive structures have been described in game theory, a scientific field that received more attention with the book Theory of Games and Economic Behavior in 1944 and the works of John Forbes Nash on non-cooperative games.

I believe we can do it; I believe you can do it and your efforts prove that we truly are *One Sacred Band Or Society Of Friends and Brothers, Among Whom No Contention Should Ever Exist, But That Noble Contention or Rather Emulation, Of Who Can Best Work Or Best Agree* ...

Acknowledgments

I would like to thank Worshipful Brother Art Redmond and Worshipful Brother Rick Smith for giving me my first opportunity to contribute to my Mother Lodge. It seems like so many years ago that I wrote a letter to Art, and he invited me up to the Lodge to meet with some of the Brothers. I cannot thank him or Rick enough for taking a chance and letting me contribute.

I would like to thank RW-elect Brother T. Foster for the work he does in increasing the awareness of Masonry across the jurisdiction of Maryland. The investment of your time ensures there are West Gates for the men of tomorrow to knock upon.

I have so many to thank . I would be remiss if I did not thank my wife for allowing me to spend my time at this activity of Masonry. Without her understanding and support I would never have done any of these Masonic activities and had that happened I likely would not be the man I am today.

I would like to thank MW Brother R.P. Neagele for supporting me in all my Masonic endeavors, and RW Brother David Sandy for helping with the editing of this text. Thank you RW Brother F. Spicer for encouraging me to write and encouraging me not to give up on Masonry. I also owe a personal debt of thanks to Worshipful Brother Mike Codori for a kind word of advice he offered that changed my life. Mike is the only Brother in my Masonic experience who whispered good counsel reminding me that I could stretch myself too thin and that I could bite off more than I could chew, and his advice has flowed through my entire life. His reminder of the limits of our 24-inch gauge is the type of applied Masonry that men join the fraternity to receive and the type of mouth to ear investment of wisdom in another Brother that Masonry promises but so seldom delivers. Mike is a Masons Mason and I hope to be able to continue to follow his example and pay forward his advice to my Brothers by being the man that I needed.

Addendum: Sample Ten Year Lodge Plan

Palestine Lodge 2018-2028

Knowing where we are going is contingent on understanding where we are, and the challenges that are on our immediate horizon. This document shall consist of a summary of the situation and strategy, our community, externalities, near/long term recommendations, and a conclusion.

Our Environment

Catonsville is a vibrant small town, with younger couples moving in and starting families yet over the past several years we have seen new membership inquiries slow, so where are all the petitions?

The 21228-zip code is a desirable area with good schools. The average age of the residents is ~39.1 years old and males make up, so Catonsville at first glance appears to be a good fit for fraternalism, however demographics (our own and our communities) require planning and strategic action on our part to preserve Catonsville Masonry through the 21st Century.

Our Challenge

In 1955 a fortune 500 company could expect to be in business for 75 years, in 2017 the fortune 500 can expect to be in business for 15 years.

The world has changed, and this change is permanent.

The expectations of Gen X and Millennials are based on a subscription economy. They don't pay for movies or music, they stream it. They expect ongoing value for their time. They expect memorable experiences, and they expect relationships. If your product or organization does not deliver on these expectations, they will not tell you they are disappointed, they will vote with their feet.

That level of change, and service seems impossible to deliver. But Palestine needs to focus not on what it cannot do but what it can do but what it can provide that nobody else can.

Applied Masonry

In our ritual we describe two types of Masonry
- Operative masonry - the building of structures

- Speculative masonry - Using the tools and emblems of the builder's trade to build moral character

There are no new Masons in Lodge rooms, if we conflate good Masonry with good Lodge attendance, we are putting the mechanics of the fraternity ahead of its ends.

We must practice applied Masonry. This applied Masonry is practicing Brotherly Love, Relief, and Truth in the world. This is how we will form relationships with men looking for what we have to offer. What we do in the Lodge room is a dress rehearsal, we need to be seen being Masons, and practicing the fraternal bond.

Our Strategy

To successfully attract and retain men in the 21st Century we need to focus on them and how Masonry can align with their goals. This will require the Lodge to practice putting the man first. To succeed and grow we must approach the world, and every man who we meet with two questions:

3. Whence Came You? - Who is the candidate and where are they coming from?
4. What Came You Here to Do? - What are their expectations and what are they looking for?

Palestine needs to begin the relationship with a potential new member by focusing on how we can help them find those things, and if we cannot help them have the integrity to refer them to someone who can.

Through our ritual we can provide an experience like no other, we must continue to provide an excellent experience.

Through our Brothers we can provide real friendships in a world of single serving friends.

We must not conflate attending Lodge with being a good Mason; it is integral for us to practice actual applied Masonry, because there are no new Masons in Lodge rooms.

Consider this: After the battle of Opequon, McKinley accompanied a surgeon to visit a Confederate soldier taken prisoner at the battle. McKinley stated:

Almost as soon as we passed the guard, I noticed that the doctor shook hands with several Confederate prisoners. He also took from his pocket a roll of bills and distributed all he had among them. Boy-like, I looked on in wonderment; I did not know what it meant. On the way back to our camp I asked him, "Did you know these men or ever see them before?" "No," replied the doctor, "I never saw them before." "But how did you know them and why did you give them money?", I asked. "They are Masons, and we Masons have ways of finding that out." "But" I persisted, "you gave them a lot of money, all you had about you. Do you ever expect to get it back?" "Well," said the doctor, "if they are ever able to pay it back, they will. But it makes no difference to me. They are brother Masons in trouble, and I am only doing my duty." I said to myself, "If that is Masonry, I will take some of it myself."

If men are looking for friends, if they are looking for something bigger than themselves our strategy is to show those facets of the fraternity to them.

Our strategy is succinctly Masonry practiced in plain view.
Our strategy is to put the Brother at the center of what we do.

A Lodge is a number of Brethren, the building is where we confer degrees, and the world is where we practice Masonry.

Palestine Today:

Our current membership number is: 190
We have had one Brother called from labor and one Brother passed to the Degree of Fellowcraft
Out of the 58 Brothers receiving their Master Mason Degree, seven are Catonsville residents the remaining 88% of the Brothers are from the surrounding zip codes. Out of our total membership only ~16.2% resides within Catonsville the remaining 83% reside outside of 21228, 74.8% of our membership live within the state of Maryland.

Looking at our membership mix are members are predominantly retirees, which is typical:

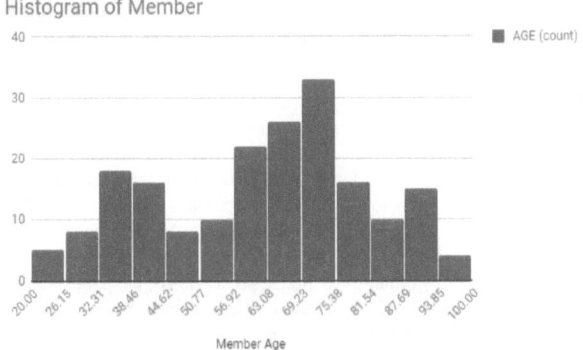

Demographics drive our future. The average life expectancy in the US is ~78.4 years old. Based on our member mix we should expect ~43.9% of our Brothers to be called from labor in the period between 2018 and 2028.

MEMBERSHIP MIX

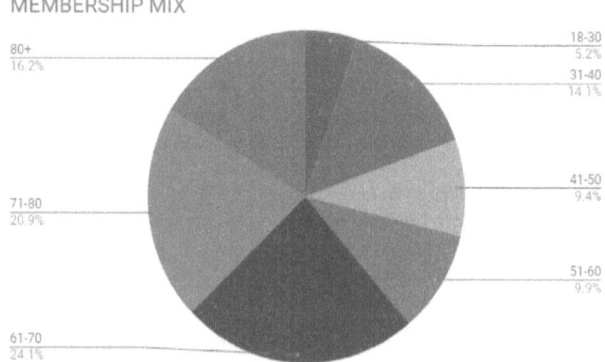

The reality is that Palestine is healthier than many Lodges in the jurisdiction and if we act now the Lodge can actively plan now to preserve Catonsville Masonry.

Membership Goals:

- Understand the community in which the Lodge resides
- Identify long term trends that may impact Lodge growth
- Identify a strategy to slowly grow membership to ensure lodge viability
    - Present engagement tactics for increasing membership
    - Identify short-term tactics to retain membership

Catonsville, MD

Catonsville has had a real estate boom, with younger couples purchasing housing stock to gain access to a safe small town with good schools at a far lower cost of entry than neighboring Howard County.

The population of our community is ~36.7k, some 47% of the population is male. With an average age of ~39 in Catonsville, first glance would have Catonsville filled with men of perfect age for Masonry.

The average age of a first-time father is now 30 years old; the parenting load does not start to decrease until the high school years. Making fathers likely to be unable to join due to parental commitments until they reach the age of 45-49 and their children do not require the same level of engagement.

Looking at the real estate trends Catonsville is desirable for young families, however the limited housing stock and later age in starting a family is creating a population of men who are likely unable to actively consider Masonry until their mid-late forties.

Catonsville has a high density of churches, and while belief in a supreme being is a requirement for joining the craft, several mainstream religious organizations actively encourage men not to join the fraternity. The most widely known is the Papal Bull discouraging Catholics from joining Freemasonry, with ~19.4% of Catonsville residents identifying as Catholic and adding Southern Baptists, 7th Day Adventists, Pentecostals, and Muslims we look at ¼ of Catonsville residents belonging to faiths which either actively discourage or may not view favorably the craft.

Taking all the variables into account the population of eligible men in Catonsville, who are unlikely to die over the next decade is: 8,760, of which 6,084 are of the ages most likely to be actively engaged in raising a family. This leaves a much-reduced target population of 2,676 men who are of the right age and unlikely to be affiliated with a religious denomination unsupportive of Freemasonry. Further, a sampling of tax records of single-family homes with 2-3 bedrooms shows them as selling at regular 4–5-year intervals, while additional research is required. Initial research suggests that young families are regularly moving making the potential target population smaller than the ~2.6k anticipated by examining the demographics.

The demographics of Catonsville have roughly ⅓ of eligible men likely to die within the next 10-15 years, ⅓ actively raising families (whom Masonry likely will not be an option). To continue viability the Lodge must seek out ways to get in front of and engage the target population of 2k men.

Target Demographic

The average age for a man to get married now is 28 years old, the average age to start a family is 31. Any membership program must deliver on the experience expected. Given that most members polled made some reference to making friends the Lodge's ability to deliver on this experience will be best done by focusing on men in their late forties who have less of a parenting burden, and those men who are reaching 65-68 who find themselves with no community as they move from the world of professional work life to retirement. Men in their twenties will move an average of 11 times in their lifetimes and may not be retained. While men in the ages between 28-31 will likely start families, it would be advisable to target those men who are not married or childless via Facebook advertising to attract these potential long-term members.

Commute Time

Reviewing the sign in book at Palestine for the past decade reveals two trends, attendance rarely exceeds 10% of our membership. Outside of the Past Masters of the Lodge, the Brothers who attend live an average of ~15 minutes' drive from the Lodge.

In our Metro area the average commute is anywhere from 30-45 minutes each way. Non-retired Members have already spent between 1 and 1.5 hours in a car prior to their commute to Lodge. This would create a circumference of membership, with the Lodge in the center. And extending to Ellicott City, Catonsville, Halethorpe, Arbutus, and Columbia.

Internet Trends

Over the past several years the Grand Lodge of Maryland has been actively advertising across the state, this and the Grand Lodge investment in Websites and social media has created an environment where men who would have located Palestine are more easily locating the MWGL of MD. This is good for the craft; however the Grand Lodge parses their inquiries and sends them out to the constituent Lodges based on the geographical location of the inquirer. Palestine has over the past decade gained brothers from outside of Catonsville, with 50% of them being introduced to Palestine by a friend or family member and the remainder locating the Lodge by finding us online. There is a direct correlation in the decrease in Palestine's web petitioners and the improvement of the Grand Lodge's web efforts and the implementation of their referral program. Unless the Grand Lodge changes their web strategy the internet shall not be a major membership driver for the foreseeable future.

It would be advisable to review the web presence and consider its intention. Members are probably not going to go to the Lodge to learn about the Lodge. The more effective marketing approach would be to have any web presence be focused on the potential new member and provide picture rich stories about how men in our target demographics have realized the values we have identified as our cultural touchstones.

For example, a photo selection of a Brother in his thirties and a man in his sixties on a page discussing the traditions of the Lodge. A photo selection of a Dad in his forties on a page discussing being part of something larger than themselves. A photo selection of Brothers of all ages discussing the fraternal aspects of the craft.

A series of landing pages should be created interviewing a handful of Brothers of all backgrounds discussing why they came to the fraternity, what they expected, and why they stay.

A contact us link that has some mystery such as: Could Masonry be for you? Or Interested, every journey begins with a first step. This should be the link that most draws the eye.

"A wealth of information creates a poverty of attention ..." —*Herbert A. Simon*

Who we are and how we can help a potential Brother meet his goals is the only message that matters? Any content that does not support membership is superfluous. Lists of Officers and Past Masters do not provide value to the man who is looking for something in Masonry and are focused on the Lodge and not the potential candidate.

When a man comes to our site looking for friendship and to be part of a tradition bigger than himself this should be exactly what they find. Palestine's history and traditions should all be presented in such a way as to support the intentions of the potential member coming to the site.

Due to the number of men moving in and out of our immediate area a special visitors section would be advisable that would invite traveling Masons to our Lodge, discuss the meeting times, and tell the visiting Brother what they should bring with them. The call to action should be: Welcome Brother - Contact us to coordinate a visit.

Membership Strategy

The Lodge needs to hold onto its current members and grow large enough to remain viable. Viability is not the same a size, to avoid membership crashes in the future the Lodge has to grow no larger than the community can support, conceivably big enough to fund programs but small enough that one Brother could conceivably know every other member. Were the Lodge to grow over 300 members, it is likely time to form another Lodge to avoid future membership crunches that threaten the Lodge's existence.

To be successful the Lodge will push itself out into the community to make men **aware** of Masonry. The burden for this will largely fall on younger men, because the Lodge needs to project itself as a mirror that potential members can see themselves in. If men want to make friends through the fraternal aspects of Masonry and be part of something bigger than themselves that is what we need to project.

The Lodge will specifically **target and engage** men in different life stages to bring them to the fraternity.

The Lodge will **retain** its members by continuing to provide programs they show interest in and reaching out to Brothers from out of state.

Not everyone who knocks gets in, not every man is going to get something out of Masonry and far fewer are going to be worth investing our finite resources in.

NEAR TERM TACTICS

Using Grand Lodge inquiries and interests from the community the Lodge's goal would be to bring in an equal number of men as Masons as we lose to Non-payment of dues or death. The Brothers under 50 must actively look to produce a number of petitions equal to the number of men whom we would anticipate being called from labor over the next decade.

2. Identify our Lodge Culture. I would recommend focusing on fellowship and ritual. A large percentage of the brethren identified making friends as their motivation to join as well as being part of something bigger than themselves. These are aspects that the Lodge can deliver on if Palestine plans activities with them in mind.
3. Identify what we want the Lodge to look like in the future. Because most of our target audience only has a vague idea that Masonry even exists the Lodge can paint its own narrative. The Lodge identifying fellowship and ritual as key attributes should create a web presence that is not focused on the Lodge, rather focused on the men coming to the Lodge.
4. Focus on Columbia and Ellicott City as potential sources of membership. The population of each area is larger than Catonsville however the mix of housing in terms of single-family homes, multi-tenant housing, and townhomes as well as the number of unmarried or divorced men of all ages makes these communities potential hot spots for Masonry.
   3. Engagement should be in the form of being seen in the community. For the unmarried man, these areas are suitcase communities so the Lodge's time would be better spent having masons meet in areas where men frequent
   4. Facebook advertising to these areas would also be recommended. This advertising would take the form of keywords.
      1. A poll amongst the under 50 Brothers as well as the 65-68 cohort would be needed. The survey would ask them to describe themselves and their interests in single words. I.e. sports, history, philosophy. Facebook will allow us to micro target the desired audience for a very moderate cost ($20 a quarter)

1.   It has been increasingly difficult to connect with interested men and have them visit the Lodge. If we coordinate monthly meet ups that rotate through Ellicott City, Columbia, and Old Ellicott City the Lodge can invite men expressing interest to meet us on their own territory and form a relationship with us early on. Asking the gentleman to come to the building is convenient for us and does not put his experience first.

b.   These meetups, not taking place on Lodge nights, could engage the Brothers who might not be interested in the Lodge experience but are interested in the fraternal experience.

c.   These meet ups would provide a venue for us to interface with Masons already living in the area, and their friends, again forming a relationship with them and making it easier for them to see Masonry as an interesting endeavor.

1.   The traveling man, or the Mason passing through, or newly moving into the area is an underserved demographic. There are several corporate headquarters in the Columbia area as well as a proximity to Ft Meade, if we optimize our web presence to be easy to locate and easy to interface with, we can effectively publicize ourselves to the world and capture new members who are already Masons but are new to the area.

1.   There are 76 members under 50 that are located within the state of Maryland, these Brothers must be encouraged to replace themselves plus one over the course of the coming decade when we will see a potential cohort of ~43.9% of the membership called from labor.

1.   The Brothers between 60 and 68, should be actively asked to talk to their friends and relatives approaching retirement, positioning Masonry as an activity to get them out of their house as a potential source of Masons.

1.   The Lodge must let every Brother know that they are entitled to a Masonic memorial service allowing the Lodge the opportunity to show its appreciation to the family of a departed Brother and leave a positive impression on the male relatives who may consider

1.   Retain our existing Brethren by continuing activities that interest them and continue to provide information on Lodge activities to the out of state Brethren to connect them to the Lodge.

1.   Engage in a Facebook marketing campaign to publicize the Lodge in Catonsville, Ellicott City, Columbia to expose potential members to the Lodge. Designed in compliance with the Grand Lodge's guide.

1.   Expand the scholarship program to include Member's children/grandchildren who are entering a graduate program. To gain exposure to additional potential membership.

LONG TERM TACTICS

If the young Masons can stabilize the membership over the coming decade, it is incumbent on the Lodge to create a stream of candidates from the community that surrounds the Lodge, this is a much longer-term problem and will require consistent effort over the next several Worshipful Masters of Palestine Lodge to effectively execute.

2.   Since the Local Community still has a large cohort of men who are eligible for petitioning the Lodge must be seen in the community and become seen as an active member of the community.
1.   4th of July Parade
2.   Chamber of Commerce

1.   Continue with the CHIP program but get the CHIP program at the schools. Partnering with the elementary schools that would put us in front of the families of men who are of potential joining age. This puts the craft in front of them while they are raising their families making them aware of us when they exit their child raising years.

1.   Engaging UMBC's student population, most graduates of the University of Maryland System stay in the state of Maryland and there are some 7,446 undergraduate males and ~1,200 male graduate students.

1.   Open the building - The Holding company and Lodge should work to locate groups that serve the families of our target members and see if the Lodge can be opened to them.

Conclusion

The Catonsville area is a challenging one and will take longer term vision to engage and create a steady stream of candidates from the 21228-zip code. In the short term the younger members must be encouraged to replace themselves to stabilize membership and buy the Lodge time to cultivate a relationship with the greater Catonsville area that provides a stream of candidates. By continued execution of the plan, and changing it as the situation changes, the Lodge can organically sustain itself and avoid membership crunches in the future. I would recommend that the Worshipful Master select a cohort of younger Masons and Past Masters and create a standing committee on long-term membership. It would be recommended that the immediate two Past Master and the Senior and Junior Warden be required committee members to ensure continuity. It would be further recommended that a long-term membership committee be a requirement spelled out in the by-laws to ensure the effort does not get forgotten as leadership changes.

To be effective the membership plan needs to put the candidate first, and match what we can provide (tradition in terms of ritual and fraternalism for example) with their expectations. Not all Masons want to come to Lodge, we need to push Masonry out into the communities that our potential Brothers live and form relationships with them.

Our Strategy

To successfully attract and retain men in the 21st Century we need to focus on them and how Masonry can align with their goals. This will require the Lodge to practice putting the man first. To succeed and grow we must approach the world, and every man who we meet with two questions:

1. Whence Came You? - Who is the candidate and where are they coming from?
1. What Came You Here to Do? - What are their expectations and what are they looking for?

Palestine needs to begin the relationship with a potential new member by focusing on how we can help them find those things by putting them first

Addendum: Detailed Catonsville Male Population Analysis

Population In Households In Catonsville	
Total Population:	36,743
Male Population:	17,445
Under 5 years:	1,067
5 to 9 years:	1,078
10 to 14 years:	1,101
15 to 17 years:	726
18 and 19 years:	396
20 years:	254
21 years:	247
22 to 24 years:	706
25 to 29 years:	1,088
30 to 34 years:	1,090
35 to 39 years:	1,015
40 to 44 years:	1,178

45 to 49 years:	1,345
50 to 54 years:	1,455
55 to 59 years:	1,288
60 and 61 years:	409
62 to 64 years:	578
65 and 66 years:	269
67 to 69 years:	363
70 to 74 years:	443
75 to 79 years:	395
80 to 84 years:	433
85 years and over:	521

Addendum: Survey Questions

2018 Palestine Membership Survey
Please take the time to complete our 2018 Membership Survey. The survey is
anonymous and will help the Lodge improve.
* Required

Why did you join the Lodge? *

Family Member was a Mason
Friend was a Mason
Community involvement
Chance to meet new friends
Open House
Popular culture
Shriner's Children's Hospitals
Esoteric reasons
Advertising

Are you active in the Lodge?

Yes
No

If you are active, why?

Your answer

If you do not make it to Lodge, why?

Your answer

What could the Lodge do to make the Lodge more interesting?

Your answer

What could the Lodge do to make the Lodge more welcoming?

Your answer

Is Masonic Education Interesting to you? (on a sliding scale of 1 being not interesting to 5 being remarkably interesting)

1
2
3
4
5

Are social events interesting to you? (on a sliding scale of 1 being not interesting to 5 being remarkably interesting)

1
2
3
4
5

Are family events interesting to you? (on a sliding scale of 1 being not interesting to 5 being remarkably interesting)

1
2
3
4
5

Is degree work interesting to you? (on a sliding scale of 1 being not interesting to 5 being remarkably interesting)

1
2
3
4
5

What is the purpose of Freemasonry?

Your answer

Does our Lodge meet your expectations as to the purpose of Freemasonry?

Yes
No

Are you willing to discuss this survey?
If you are willing to discuss this survey, please
email cXXXXXXXX@gmail.com

Yes
No

"There's no that there! This old chestnut gets a laugh in every Masonic Lodge. Our success is going to be tied to the discovery of the next Masonic punchline with an equally universal appeal... and making the men who are going to discover it equally hilarious in the eyes of our Brethren"

Charles Matulewicz

About the Author

Born outside of Camden, New Jersey Charles attended Temple University's
Tyler School of Art where he studied Art History as an undergraduate. He
furthered his education by obtaining an M.B.A. from Texas A&M, and a post
Graduate Certificate in Marketing from Harvard University. He currently
resides in Oella, Maryland with his wife Amanda in a home slightly older than
the war between the states with two greyhounds where he is working to finish
a M.S. in Nonprofit Management from LSU and still struggles to not wake his
wife up when returning from a Lodge visit.

Charles served as Worshipful Master of Palestine Lodge No.189 and the
Maryland Masonic Lodge of Research No.239. He is a frequent contributor to
Maryland's Scottish Rite and Grand Lodge publications. Charles has served in
leadership positions in several appendant bodies. He has served the Grand
Lodge of Maryland in several appointed and leadership capacities. He
eschews titles and lapel pins. If you are traveling in Maryland, you have a
high probability of running into him at a random Masonic meeting somewhere
in the state…

www.ingramcontent.com/pod-product-compliance
Lightning Source LLC
Chambersburg PA
CBHW030642220526
45463CB00004B/1605